# Clever
# Party Planning

We invite you to share in the joy, spirit, and
peace of the angels by finding all 29
of them throughout this book!

# Clever
# Party Planning

*Party planning ideas and themes for
kids, teens and adults*

## Suzanne Singleton

Twenty-Nine
Angels *Publishing*

Printed in the USA.

FIRST EDITION

10  9  8  7  6  5  4  3  2  1

Singleton, Suzanne.
    Clever Party Planning. Summary: a handbook of party planning ideas and themes for children, teenagers, and adults; party tips.

ISBN 0-9661253-2-0
Library of Congress Catalog Card Number: 99-90534

Cover illustration and photography, and book design:
Nancy Johnston, Brushwood Graphics, Inc.

Interior illustrations:
Linda Ports, LP Design & Visual Communications

Editing:
Bonnie Stecker
Paula Molino
Donna Babylon
    Windsor Oak Publishing
    author of **More Splash Than Cash Decorating Ideas**

Proofing:
Gina Molino

I dedicate these pages to my Italian family of two sisters, a brother, my parents, cousins, aunts and uncles, and my precious Nonna, each of whom has been a guest at my home for a multitude of family festivities. Also, to each of my playful party chums . . . great thanks for mobbing my house with merriment, affection, joking, and a gigantic mess!

You may have offered one idea
You may have offered many,
But surely this book wouldn't be as thick
If you hadn't offered any!

My thanks, friends! Your input means quite a lot!

Donna Babylon
Stacey Brooks
Becky Crist
Terese Cashen
Barb Ford
Tamar Fleishman
Hubs
Sue Hanley
Diane Hock
Dinah Kappus
Mom & Dad,
   the party originators
Nancy Mugele

Pamela Molino,
   my little sister
Paula Molino,
   my big sister
Stuart & Alicia Matthai
Bernadette Moyer,
   author of **Angel Stacey**
Bill Mahoney
Jim Mossa
Linda McLeod
Linda Ports
Marge Steele
Bonnie Stecker

# The Parties

## table of contents

# Introduction

I love throwing parties. I love filling my house with plenty of friends. And I like being clever about it. Maybe my desire to plan a lot of parties has something to do with me being in the spotlight (I like it!). Or, maybe because it simply delights me to be around happy, upbeat people and the way I can do that is to invite them over!

Many ideas and tips written in this book are ones that I have actually accomplished in my party planning career. (The best being the tethered hot air balloon rides in our backyard during my husband's surprise FIFTY PLUS ONE party!) Others I hope to implement one day, and some ideas I'll never get to, but still, I think they are good. (Of course, now my friends are really going to expect a lot out of my future parties after reading this book!)

I tried not to make the planning too challenging for you. I want you to be able to browse through the book, pick an idea and say "I can do that," without feeling that any idea is beyond your talents or scope. My illustrator even provided you with invitation templates, instructions, and envelope sizes for most of the kids' theme parties. While looking through other party books to plan my kids' birthday parties, I wasn't confident that I could make that beautiful two-tiered, three color castle cake, equipped with drawbridge and towers. Put it this way—mine would have never looked like the picture! Let's be real. Who has time nowadays to get fancy? I think you will like the ideas and themes presented in the kids' section. In each category of each theme, I offer not just one idea, but several, so you can pick the idea just right for your child's party and appropriate for his age.

In creating ideas, I also thought about readers' budgets, thus naming some ideas which are inexpensive to produce and others which are more elaborate.

The teen section should be very helpful to a lot of parents. Have you ever seen a party book geared for the teenager? That chapter was added after a friend pointed out that I had covered kids' themes and adult parties, but not teens. She was right! Party planning for teenagers can be challenging. They can be a bunch hard to please and easy to bore.

After reading **Clever Party Planning**, I hope you will never be at a loss for an idea when planning a special party for a special someone in your life. At the most, reading these ideas may spark your creativity for your own ideas! Just have fun planning. And remember . . . be clever!

# Kids' Party
# Reasons
# for the Seasons

Party themes and ideas
for ages 3 to 11 including suggestions for invitations,
costumes, decorations, games, activities,
crafts, food, cake and favors

# What We Learn From Children

What we learn from children
It may surprise you so.
They're quite the little teachers,
More than we'll ever know.

We've learned that stickers on the furniture
Can be easily removed.
And that a safety scissors haircut
Can't always be approved.

We've learned that "Not Me"
is a mysterious friend to all.
That kid will always show up,
Without us having to call.

Painting the door with orange sherbet,
Markers or some other kind of goo,
Is no need for a total upset,
There are better things to do.

We've learned the pleasures of night-time stories,
And cuddles in the bed.
Holding hands for a walk in the park,
And loving kisses on the head.

We've learned to enjoy dandelion bouquets,
While holding back an allergic sneeze.
And place them in a pretty vase,
Knowing our child has tried to please.

Children teach us patience,
Though not always easy to display.
Among toothless grins and tempers,
We've learned to count and walk away.

When low moments are here, remember they go,
As quickly as they came.
So don't sweat the small stuff,
Forever memories are what you'll gain.

Just hold on tight and celebrate,
The joyful times you've made.
What we learn from children
Are precious moments to be saved.

by Jackie Seal-Levin
Director
Chestnut Ridge Grace Preschool
Reisterstown, Maryland

I t's your child's birthday. You want to produce the happiest birthday kid alive, right? What a challenge! Plan a wonderful day of fun that your child will always remember by choosing from one of these 32 themes and additional party ideas. This chapter will help simplify your task of organizing a delightful party—one that will please you, the guests, and most importantly, your child.

Check out all of the ideas before making your final plans because in most categories, more than one idea is presented. You may want to mix and match ideas, using a game from one theme, a food suggestion from another theme, and an invitation design from a third.

If age appropriate, involve your child in the planning and preparation so that it will be his party and not yours. Whatever type of party you invent, remember that kids enjoy the anticipation of the upcoming birthday as much as party day itself. They will most likely have a great time at any kind of party because they are the focus of attention.

# Flower Power

**Wow them with flowers!**
**This springtime birthday party is bursting with the**
**colors of a freshly planted flower garden.**

PLEASE COME TO
·A·
**FLOWER POWER**
PARTY

Buzz on over
to Megan's house to
celebrate her 5th birth-
day on March 12th
2pm- 4pm

RSVP
Barb 555-6789

## The Invitation

**Paper Flower**—What better indication of springtime than a buzzing bee inside of a flower? Cut out a construction paper flower shape and fold it in half. Add construction paper leaves and a stem. Party details will be written inside of the flower and can be seen when the flower's flap is folded down. Add a bee inside of the flower (draw it or use a sticker). See template, page 170.

Felt Vase—Make a vase out of felt (two vase shapes glued together along the borders). Make individual construction paper flowers and stick them inside of the vase. A party detail can be written on each flower.

## What to Wear

To add vibrant springy colors to this party, invite guests to wear flowered clothing and accessories, or clothes adorned with bees and colorful butterflies.

## Decoration Ideas

Tablecloth—Kids will be buzzing around the party table covered with a flowered tablecloth or a large piece of flowered fabric. For placemats, cut out large flower shapes from various colors of paper placemats (found in party stores). Or, cut out large flowers from flower print contact paper and stick them onto paper placemats.

Fresh Flowers—Add a springtime aroma with vases of fresh flowers. Use as a centerpiece, and place them on the coffee table, in the kitchen, on the buffet table, around the party area, even in the powder room.

Decorate the guests!—Adorn their hair with fresh flowers held by bobby pins or cute barrettes in the shape of a bee, flower, or butterfly.

Flower Face—Draw a huge, colorful flower on a large piece of foam board. Cut out the middle of the flower. Take instant pictures as guests place their faces through the hole. Give the photos as party favors.

Gardening Garnishes—Use painted watering cans as decor, placed beside flatbeds of flowers just waiting to be planted. Add gardening tools and gloves for a finishing touch.

## Games & Activities To Play and Do

Tablecloth Making—Like bees are attracted to flowers, attract your guests to the table by asking them to draw on the tablecloth! Cover the party table with white butcher paper and instruct the children to draw and color bunches of flowers and spring scenes.

**Face Paint**—Each guest can have a colorful flower or butterfly painted on her cheek.

**Thumbprint Flowers**—Give each guest a piece of white paper and have them use a colorful stamp pad to make thumbprint flower petals. Then instruct them to draw and color stems and leaves to complete their unique flower creations.

**Does He Love Me?**—Remember as a kid picking apart flowers while reciting, "He loves me, He loves me not?" Provide flowers for the girls to pick off the petals to see if they have found true love!

**Pin the Bee**—Using a felt board, play Pin the Bee on the Flower using the same game rules as Pin the Tail on the Donkey. Make the pieces out of felt.

**Follow that Flower**—With safety pins, secure white pieces of drawing paper to every child's back and give everyone a bright colored crayon or marker. Line up the party guests. A parent leads the group around the room (also with a piece of paper on her back), while everyone tries to draw a flower on the paper in front of her. A guaranteed giggler!

## Craft Options

**Tissue Paper Flowers**—Layer several pieces of large colored tissue paper. Fold them accordion style. Tie the middle of the stack with a pipe cleaner which serves as the flower's stem. One at a time, separate and fluff the layers of tissue until a blossom is formed.

**Painted Pots**—Provide everyone with paints and small clay flower pots. Have them paint the pots and set aside to dry. Later, have everyone fill the pots with dirt. Provide flower seeds or potted petunias for each guest to plant.

**Gardening Gloves**—Using fabric markers, personalize plain canvas gardening gloves with names and flower artwork. Sequins and gems can be added, too.

**Coffee Filter Flower**—Paint coffee filters with watercolors. When dry, push green pipe cleaners through the center for the stem. Draw the center of the flower, and add a small fabric bumblebee on a wire (look in craft stores).

**Peanut Bee**—Paint peanut shells yellow with black stripes to make bumblebees. Glue on tissue paper wings and small movable eyes.

**Clothes Pin Butterfly**—Stack several sheets of small pieces of colored tissue paper (precut in shape of butterfly wings). Use painted wooden clothes pins to pinch the middle of the tissue paper stack to form the butterfly's body. On the clothes pin, glue on movable eyes and small pieces of pipe cleaner for the antennae.

**Sunny Sunflower**—Glue sunflower seeds all over a yellow paper plate. Glue short pieces (3") of yellow crepe paper around the edges of the plate so they extend to resemble the sunflower's petals. For the stem, paint a paper towel roll green and hot glue it to the back of the plate. Glue green construction paper leaves to the paper towel roll.

## Food & Treat Selections

**Flower Power Food!**—Use a can of squirt cheese to form flower designs on round crackers.

**Cheese Flowers**—Cut out pieces of cheese using a small flower cookie cutter. Add thin slices of celery for the flower stems and place cheese and celery together on a rectangular cracker.

**Sweet Butterflies**—Make a batch of sugar cookies in the shape of butterflies. Remove the dough from the inside of the wings and fill with colorful crushed hard candies. When baked, the candies melt and the cookies have a stained glass effect.

## Cake Possibility

Make "dirt" dessert using chocolate pudding and crushed chocolate cookies on top. Put these in individual ice cream cone "pots." Add gummy worms or plastic flowers. Or, make this dirt dessert:

### Dirt Dessert

large container of prepared whipped topping
2—8 oz. cream cheese
2 large instant vanilla pudding
1 cup powdered sugar
3 cups milk
2 teaspoons vanilla extract
1 bag chocolate sandwich cookies
optional: 1 can cherry pie filling

Beat cream cheese and powdered sugar until smooth. Add pudding mix and milk and beat until smooth. Add whipped topping, vanilla and pie filling. Chill until set. Grind cookies in a blender. Layer cookies and creamed mixture in large clean flower pot, ending with cookie crumbs on top. Refrigerate until served. Stick in artificial flowers.

## Favors To Go

Guests will be "sniffing" around to see what colorful items they will receive as party favors. Place stuffed bees, flower tattoos, flower stickers, and butterfly barrettes in small buckets or pretty planters. Wrap in colored plastic wrap, and tie on packs of sunflower seeds with colorful pipe cleaners.

# Krazy Karnival

*Come one, come all to an old fashioned neighborhood carnival. Prizes and games galore make this Krazy Karnival hard to ignore!*

## The Invitation

**Tickets, please!**—Get the kids in the mood for this Krazy Karnival with invitations resembling tickets for a carnival ride. This can be done simply on the computer with carnival graphics, a festive font, and card stock. Make several to a page and cut. See template, page 171.

**Carnival Flyers**—Tie rolled-up flyers to the end of ribbons on helium balloons. Add small weights to each (a few pennies in a plastic sandwich bag).

## Decoration Ideas

**Carnival Booths**—Like a real carnival, this party area will be set up with carnival booths. Make the booths out of large cardboard boxes, and spray paint them different colors. Hand letter the name of the booth on a sign or on the front of the box, such as "Hot Dogs, 2 tickets," "Spin Art, 1 ticket," and "Clothespin Drop, 1 ticket." Add artwork. Hang the signs on the front of each booth or attach them to ground stakes.

**Tickets**—The kids can freely visit the booths of their choice, using carnival tickets (available in office supply and party stores). Or, you can create books of tickets on the computer with activities and treats printed on each one, such as GOOD FOR ONE COTTON CANDY, GOOD FOR A MOONBOUNCE, etc.

**Balloons**—Hang bunches of multi-colored balloons all around the yard, on the deck, and at each carnival booth.

**Tablecloth**—A perfect tablecloth for the cake table can be a multicolored polka-dotted one. Clown plates are a fun table decor for this theme and can be found easily in party stores.

## Games & Activities To Play & Do

**Prizes**—Every carnival has a slew of prizes to win! Pick one of two ways to handle the prizes:

1) Hand out popcorn boxes as treat bags (each labeled with a guest's name) to collect prizes as kids visit the booths. Ask a movie theater for a supply of popcorn boxes—the red and white striped ones with a flap lid. If you are more ambitious, sew prize bags from colorful fabric (striped or polka-dot) and close with a ribbon drawstring.

2) In lieu of prizes at each booth, award buttons, chocolate coins or bubble gum. At the end of the party, kids cash these in for toy prizes.

Have volunteer adults supervise each booth. Ideas for booths include:

**Carnival Ride**—Your money will be well spent if you rent a moonbounce for this event, or a small kiddie ride like a four-cage ferris wheel or mini carousel.

**Face Painting**—Solicit a neighborhood teen to dress up like a clown and paint faces. Draw sample artwork on poster board before the party so the kids have designs from which to choose.

**Clown Station**—Hire a clown (or ask a parent to volunteer) to teach kids how to turn themselves into one. Provide clown wigs, red noses, makeup, and a mirror.

**Fishing Pond**—Place plastic sandwich bags filled with candy in an empty kiddie pool. Tie a ribbon on each bag so it is easy to snag. Make a few fishing poles out of dowel rods, nylon thread, and an open paper clip with a weight (to keep nylon thread taut).

Award small prizes for these activities, which can be set up at individual booths:

**Bean Bag Toss**—Draw a clown on a piece of plywood or an artist's canvas (available in art supply and craft stores). Cut out a hole for the face. Use this for two purposes: 1) bean bag toss, and 2) kids stand behind it and put their faces through the hole to get pictures taken.

**Pick-A-Duck**—Write numbers on the bottom of wind-up floating toys or plastic ducks. Place them in a basin or kiddie pool filled with water. Each child picks up a toy and wins the prize related to the number on the duck.

**Clothespin Drop**—The trick is to accurately aim a clothespin so it drops into the opening of an empty gallon milk jug.

**Hole-In-One**—Provide a golf putting mat, a putter, and golf balls. A prize is awarded for a hole in one.

**Animal Bowling**—Set up 10 stuffed animals in a bowling pin configuration (4 in the back row, then 3, then 2, then 1 in the front row). To win, kids must get a spare or a strike when rolling a ball toward the animals. Make a starting line on the grass with spray paint or on the sidewalk with masking tape or chalk.

**Football Toss**—Toss a football through a basketball hoop to win a prize.

**Penny Drop**—Set up a large jar of water with a shot glass at the bottom. Kids must try to get a penny to land inside of the shot glass to win a prize.

**Pick-a-Pop**—Using green and blue markers, color the ends of some lollipop sticks, leaving some plain. Stick the lollipops in a styrofoam block. If a child picks a green or a blue lollipop stick, a prize is awarded (one for green; a different one for blue). If a child picks a plain stick, he wins the lollipop. You can have a grand prize in this game by coloring only one of the lollipop tips red. Whoever picks that lollipop wins the grand prize like a large stuffed animal.

## Craft Options

**Spin Art & Sand Art**—You've probably seen these crafts at festivals and carnivals. Kids love making them! Spin art is a machine that you can buy or rent. A piece of thick paper is placed inside of the machine on a spinning disk. Kids squirt various paint colors onto the spinning disk to create a work of art. Sand art is the craft of filling a shaped glass or plastic bottle with various layers of colored sand. These kits are available in craft stores.

**Magnetic Picture Frames**—Provide painted popsicle sticks to make a square frame, and supply beads, buttons, foam shapes and glue for frame decorations. Glue magnets on the backs of the frames so they become refrigerator magnets.

**Hat Painting**—Provide plain white painter's hats or plastic visors for kids to decorate with puffy paints, fabric markers or foam shapes.

## Food & Treat Selections

Lots of yummy treats are available at this carnival! Set up individual food stations on card tables (interspersed with the carnival booths) and decorate with an illustrated poster depicting the food. Let the birthday child illustrate the signs. Carnival food ideas include:

- miniature pizza bagels
- hot dogs
- fruit salad in cups or scooped out oranges
- popcorn in clown face bags
- soft pretzels with dips of honey mustard, icing and cinnamon
- cotton candy (rent a machine or purchase ready-made)
- jars of penny candy, individually wrapped
- cupcakes baked in ice cream cones
- peppermint sticks in lemons

- ice cream sundae bar:
    chocolate, vanilla, strawberry ice cream
    hot fudge and caramel toppings
    sprinkles
    crushed chocolate cookies or candy bars
    m&m's
    peanuts
    whipped topping
    maraschino cherries

## Cake Possibility

Order a designed cake from a bakery or use your own cake decorating skills to make a colorful carnival theme depicting a roller coaster, ferris wheel, carnival game, or a clown.

## Favors To Go

The carnival is packing up and moving on until next season! The favors for this event are the crafts and prizes collected throughout the day.

# Very Ladybug-Like!

**Ladybugs are our friends, and they're lucky, too!
Plenty of red and black spots will be dancing
before their eyes at this party!**

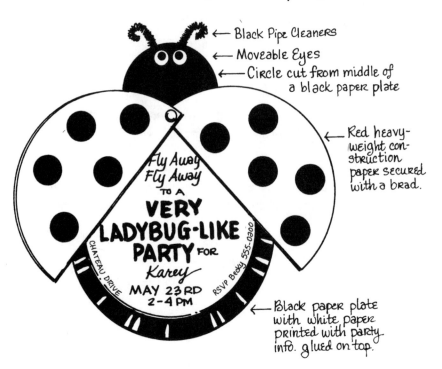

← Black Pipe Cleaners

← Moveable Eyes

← Circle cut from middle of a black paper plate

← Red heavy-weight construction paper secured with a brad.

Fly Away
Fly Away
TO A
**VERY
LADYBUG-LIKE
PARTY** FOR
*Karey*
MAY 23 RD
2-4 PM

CHATEAU DRIVE

RSVP Becky 555-0300

← Black paper plate with white paper printed with party info. glued on top.

## The Invitation

**Movable Ladybug**—This invitation will fly right into little hands to tell children when to gather for this very ladybug-like party. Use a black paper plate for the ladybug's body. To make movable wings, attach red construction paper half circles to the plate with brass fasteners. For the head, cut a circle from another black paper plate; attach moveable eyes and black pipe cleaners. With a marker, draw black spots on the wings. Write the party details on white paper and glue to plate.

**Living Ladybugs**—Purchase real ladybugs (found in hardware and lawn/garden stores) and small clear plastic boxes with lids and very small holes. Put a few ladybugs inside of each box along with an invitation of your choice.

## What to Wear

Friendly little ladybugs are invited to wear red and black clothes. As they arrive, have a parent volunteer face paint black spots on their cheeks.

## Decoration Ideas

**Tablecloth**—This is an easy party to decorate. Think red and black everything! Start with a red tablecloth. Cut out large black circles from black construction paper and place them all over the table top. Cover with clear plastic. Or, use a solid green tablecloth to simulate grass and place a bunch of ladybug illustrations under the plastic. These can be taken from a coloring book or computer graphics. Let the birthday child color them.

**Placemats**—Ladybug placemats can be constructed out of red and black stiff felt.

**Balloons**—Scatter lots of red and black non-helium balloons all over the party room, or let bunches of helium-filled balloons float to the ceiling.

## Games & Activities To Play and Do

**Free the Ladybugs!**—Buy a stock of ladybugs (as mentioned above) and celebrate with a "ladybug release," outside of course! Then go on a ladybug hunt. Provide toy magnifying glasses and jars (see craft options below).

**Storytelling**—Your role is changed to storyteller as you read "The Grouchy Ladybug" or other favorite book about ladybugs. Have the children act out the story.

Ladybug Toss—Make black beanbags and toss them through holes cut out of red foam board or artist's canvas. Using black pipe cleaners and small styrofoam balls, add large antennae to the top.

Song Scramble—Write each word of a song (a ladybug song would be appropriate, or use "Happy Birthday") on separate index cards. Make two sets. Scramble and place out of order on a table. Kids line up in two teams and take turns moving one index card at a time until the song is in order. The winning team is the first who puts the song together.

Pin the Spots—Play Pin the Spots on the Ladybug in the same way as Pin the Tail on the Donkey. Use a felt board.

## Craft Options

Ladybug Jar—Decorate the lids of small jars with red fuzzy pompons and attach small pieces of black pipe cleaners for antennae. Add movable eyes. (Use this jar for the ladybug hunt—see Activities above.)

Antennae—Attach black or red pipe cleaners to headbands. Stick small styrofoam balls on the ends of the pipe cleaners or make loops in the pipe cleaners. The kids can wear these on their heads.

Refrigerator Magnet—Kids assemble red clothespins, black felt spots (use a hole puncher), chenille pipe cleaners, and movable eyes. Glue magnets to the backs of the clothes pins.

## Food & Treat Selections

In keeping with the red and black color scheme of the party, consider serving the following food for ladybug-related treats:

- pizza adorned with halved black olives
- watermelon
- red and black licorice tray
- red gelatin with chocolate chips inside

## Cake Possibilities

A **"Lady" Bug?**—Ask a bakery to illustrate a ladybug dressed up like a "lady," with high heels, a red purse, earrings, lipstick and a pretty hat!

**Black & Red**—Make a round cake with red icing and black spots. Use black licorice for the ladybug's legs and antennae.

## Favors To Go

Kids will fly home clutching these favors! Use red lunch bags and stick on black label dots, or glue on black circles made from construction paper. Include goodies such as stuffed ladybugs, ladybug tattoos, red and black licorice, red lollipops, and storybooks about ladybugs.

# ☆Over the Rainbow

*Somewhere over the rainbow is a magical party where children are covered in marvelous colors of rainbow fun!*

## The Invitation

Just like clouds and rainbows seem suspended in the sky, so does this mobile invitation. Cut out three clouds and a rainbow arch from colored foam sheets. String one cloud and the rainbow together with nylon thread to make a mini mobile. Glue the other two clouds on each end. With a permanent marker, write on the party details. Paint the clouds with white glitter paint.

## What to Wear

Invite every color of the rainbow to this party! On the invitation, assign a rainbow color to each guest, who then has to dress in that color from head to toe. When guests arrive, paint everyone's fingernails each a different color.

## Decoration Ideas

**Rainbow Arch**—Make guests feel as if they have really arrived over the rainbow by making an arch out of multi-colored balloons or twisted crepe paper at the entrance. (Tape these to a door frame.) Play the song, "Somewhere Over The Rainbow" from the Wizard of Oz.

**Ceiling Scenery**—Clouds, suns and pots of gold can hang from the ceiling. Make these out of colored foam board and attach nylon thread for hanging.

**Tablecloth**—Select a vibrant color of the rainbow (like purple) to use for a tablecloth, then for contrast, make placemats in the shape of clouds out of white foam sheets. The napkins can be red, the cups can be yellow, and the plastic utensils can be green and orange.

**Shining Centerpiece**—A centerpiece can be a "pot of gold," made out of an inexpensive plastic gold planting pot. Spread silver glitter all over it, then load it with chocolate gold coins.

## Games & Activities To Play and Do

**Rainbow Race**—Cut large circles of various colors of construction paper. Give two to each participant. Kids must use the circles to "walk" from start to finish by placing one circle on the floor, stepping on it, then placing the other circle on the floor and stepping on that. Then they pick up one circle and place it on the floor, pick up the other, etc. making their way to the finish line.

**Search for Gold**—Around the house or yard, hide small pots of gold made out of mini yogurt containers spray painted gold and filled with chocolate coins. (Wrap the containers in plastic wrap or gold tissue paper.) Each guest must find the pot of gold with his/her name on it.

**Pan for Gold**—Set up a large basin with sand on the bottom and half filled with water. Bury a bunch of pennies in the sand. Provide plastic sifters. When the sand and water sift through, the pennies will remain in the sifter and the kids will have struck it rich! Provide gold spray painted yogurt containers or toy treasure boxes for them to collect their "gold."

**Rainbow Hunt**—Hide simple construction paper shapes like red tulips, purple butterflies, yellow suns, green grass, orange flowers, etc. Kids must find the shapes matching the same color as they are dressed for the party.

## Craft Options

**Rainbow Pin**—Cut multi-colored pipe cleaners into thirds. Place several colors together and twist. Curve into an arch shape. Glue half of a cotton ball to each end to serve as clouds. Attach a small safety pin underneath with hot glue.

**Color Collage**—Kids scribble various colors of crayons on a white piece of paper so that it makes a solid mass of integrated colors. Then, with black tempera paint, cover the entire sheet of paper to hide the colors. Have guests scratch through the black paint (when dry) with the edge of a coin to draw a rainbow or write their names. The colors will show through!

**Sand Art**—Kids fill a shaped glass or plastic bottle with layers of colored sand. Provide a separate table covered with newspaper, bottles, plastic spoons and containers of sand. Sand art kits are available in craft stores.

**T-Shirt Spraying**—Paint white T-shirts using fabric paint in spray bottles. Do this activity at the beginning of the party to allow time for the shirts to dry so the guests can take them home.

**Colorful Crayons**—Place bits of crayon pieces between two pieces of wax paper. Iron it for the kids and see something colorful happen!

## Food & Treat Selections

This menu will spark your creativity to conjure up ideas for colorful food!

**Rainbow Platter**—Make a hamburger platter using lettuce, purple cabbage, and tomatoes. Add color around the perimeter with purple and green grapes, orange slices, radishes, carrots, yellow and red peppers, and broccoli. Provide dip for the vegetables.

**Gelatin Cubes**—Make different colored gelatin in ice cube trays. When set, stick in decorative toothpicks to eat like hors d'oeuvres.

> **Treats**—Serve multi-colored treats such as:
> rainbow popsicles
> multi-colored popcorn
>    (sold in nut and candy stores)
> fruit salad
> fruit roll-ups
> colorful candy such as Skittles, Nerds, candy necklaces,
>    rainbow bubble gum, or jellybeans
> colorful cereal

Ideas for rainbow colored food and drinks:
RED—pizza, apples, punch
ORANGE—oranges, sherbet, mango, Kool-Aid
YELLOW—bananas, lemon yogurt, lemons, lemonade
GREEN—grapes, kiwi, celery, green olives, limes, Kool-Aid
BLUE—blueberry toaster pastry, blueberries, blue fruit
        drinks
PURPLE—grapes, grape juice

## Cake Possibilities

**Rainbow Cake**—Make a bundt cake, cut it in half and turn the halves over so they stand up (flat side on plate) close to each other. Decorate with icing in an arch using the colors of the rainbow. Place a pile of marshmallows at each end to resemble clouds (slightly melt them together in the microwave).

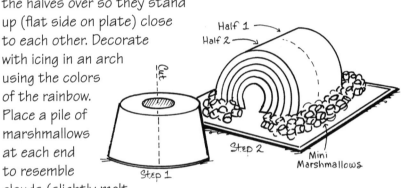

**Cupcakes**—Instead of a cake, serve cupcakes with each decorated in a different color icing.

## Favors To Go

They say at the end of every rainbow, there's a pot of gold. Let there be one at the end of this party! Make pots of gold out of small peat pots from a garden store. Fill them with chocolate coins and wrap the pots in gold tissue paper. Attach white paper clouds with pieces of raffia and write "Thanks for coming over the rainbow" in colorful letters, along with your child's signature.

# The Fishing Hole

**Kids will reel in a good time at this party.**
**Let's go down to the fishing hole**
**for the catch of the day!**

## The Invitation

Something's fishy about this party invitation. Make a fish shape out of construction paper. Glue on fish scales, made from torn pieces of colorful tissue paper. Attach a paper clip to the fish's mouth and nylon thread to the paper clip to simulate a hook and fishing line. Write the party details on various sizes of "bubbles" (blue paper) and include with the invitation. See template, page 172.

25

## What to Wear

Let the little fishermen take their party role "reel" seriously. Ask them to wear fishing vests and hats. Provide colorful (safe) lures to hang on their hats when they arrive (use cheap hook earrings in colorful designs and shapes).

## Decoration Ideas

**Net Tablecloth**—Don't let the big one get away! Over a green tablecloth, throw a large piece of netting to cover the table top. Tangle small plastic fish in the net. Placemats can be fish shaped (purchased or homemade).

**Fishing Decor**—Around the party area, set out fishing poles, tackle boxes, fishing hats, driftwood, and fish knickknacks. Hang fish party lights.

## Games and Activities To Play and Do

**Nature Hike**—Take a short walk to a nearby pond, lake or stream. Try to spot fish and tadpoles.

**Fishing Demo**—Have an adult demonstrate the use of a fishing pole and how to bait the hook. Let the kids take a practice turn tossing out and reeling in the line.

**Go for the Goldfish**—Set up a kiddie pool with water and place real goldfish inside. Provide small fish nets for kids to catch the fish, then send the fish home in sturdy plastic bags.

**Pond of Candy**—Place plastic sandwich bags filled with candy in an empty kiddie pool. Tie a ribbon on each bag so it is easy to snag. Make fishing poles out of dowel rods, nylon thread, and an open paper clip with a weight (to keep nylon thread taut).

**Card Game**—Play "Go Fish."

## Craft Options

**Bait Box**—Decorate small plastic containers by gluing on candy fish. Fill with gummy worms.

**Tackle Boxes**—Egg cartons make the perfect tackle box for little fishermen. Craft handles from several pipe cleaners twisted together. Fill with goldfish crackers, toy frogs, and gummy worms.

## Food & Treat Selections

**Tuna Salad**—The perfect food to serve at this fishing party. For miniature tuna fish sandwiches, cut the bread in the shape of a fish, using a fish cookie cutter if you have one.

**A Fishy Dessert**—Inside of a new fish bowl, place colored candy at the bottom to simulate colored rocks. Add blueberry gelatin to fill most of the fish bowl (simulates water). Add gummy fish throughout when gelatin is beginning to set.

**Goldfish Crackers**—a perfect addition to this party table and a yummy snack!

## Cake Possibility

No need to order this cake. It's a do-it-yourselfer! Either draw a simple fish shape with icing on a rectangular cake, or cut a fish shape out of the cake, then add icing. Use three cupcakes with blue icing to simulate bubbles floating up from the fish's mouth.

## Favors To Go

Don't let the kids slip away without a fishy favor! Since they are taking home real goldfish (see games and activities above), favors can be placed inside of small fish bowls, with fish food and directions on how to care for goldfish. (Make sure you mention that they usually live only for a short time.) You can also stick one or two of the following inside of the fish bowl: toy amphibians such as frogs, tadpoles, and fish, or the card game 'Go Fish.'

# Summer You're Buggin' Me!

### Bugs, Bugs Everywhere!
*These pesty creatures crawl, fly, and nest their way into this party for creepy crawly fun!*

← Cut out a circle from top of invitation. Tape or glue mylar on inside.

← FOLD

← Add construction paper bugs, computer clip art insects or creepy crawlers cut from magazines.

## The Invitation

**Magnifying Glass**—Guests will clearly read the details of this party! Cut out a magnifying glass shape from black paper. Use clear plastic wrap or clear Mylar paper to represent the glass of the magnifier. The party details will be on a separate piece of paper underneath so it looks like the words are magnified. With these invitations, include small plastic bugs. See template, page 173.

**Bug Spray**—For a hand delivered invitation, make fake bug spray cans out of clean orange juice cans. Wrap colored paper around the cans and write "Bug Spray" across them. Roll up invitations and place inside the can with a few plastic bugs.

## What to Wear

"Buggy" is the way to be for this party, so ask guests to wear bug T-shirts. Provide antennae for everyone by making them out of headbands and pipe cleaners, or purchase them from a novelty or party store.

## Decoration Ideas

**Tablecloth**—Catch the bugs with the largest net around—the one thrown over a dark green tablecloth. Stick large plastic bugs through the net. For placemats, cut large leaf shapes out of green construction paper.

**Ceiling Scenery**—Hang paper bugs from the ceiling and tape them to the floor.

**Icy Bugs**—Make trays of ice cubes with bug candy frozen inside.

## Games & Activities To Play and Do

**Musical Bugs**—Play this game like musical chairs. Pictures of bugs are taped to the floor of the party room (have one less than the number of guests). Everyone marches around when the music starts. When it stops, kids must stand on a bug. Remove one bug. Let the child who missed the cue start and stop the music for the next turn, until another child misses. Remove another bug. Continue until only one person is left standing on one bug.

**What Bug Am I?**— Kids sit in a circle. Glue pictures and names of different bugs on index cards. One child picks a card, and the others try to guess the bug, taking turns asking yes and no questions (Does it have four legs? Is it green? Does it bite?) Or, safety pin to each guest's back a bug picture and name. The kids have to ask each other yes or no questions during the party to figure out what bug is crawling on his or her own back.

**ABC Bug Hunt**—In an alphabetical format, the first person in the circle says, "I went on a bug hunt and I found an Ant." The next person in the circle says, "I went on a bug hunt and I found an Ant and a Beetle." The third kid says, "I went on a bug hunt and I found an Ant, a Beetle and a Cricket." Use each letter of the alphabet, reciting every bug named each time around. This is a good memory test and a bit challenging! Here are a few suggestions so adults can assist:

A — ant, aphid
B — beetle, bee, bedbug, black widow
C — cricket, carpenter ant, centipede
D — damsel fly, daddy long leg
E — earwig
F — fly, firefly, flea
G — grasshopper
H — honeybee, hornet, horsefly
I — insect, ice bug
J — Jerusalem cricket, June beetle
K — katydid
L — lightening bug, ladybug, locust
M — mosquito, moth, maggot
N — nymph
O — oil beetle
P — praying mantis
Q — queen bee
R — roach
S — spider, silkworm, stick insect
T — termite, tick, tarantula
U — ugly bug
V — vespoid wasp
W — wasp, worm, weevil
X — xyelid sawfly
Y — yellow jacket
Z — zootermopsis (termite)

**Bug Bingo**—Make up bingo cards with B-U-G-S written across the top and names of bugs in each square of the bingo card. Mix up the squares on each card, that is, do not make each bingo card the same. As bug names are called out, the kids can mark the appropriate space on the bingo card with bug stickers or bingo markers. This game is won like regular bingo.

**Push-A-Bug**—Paint a few peanut shells to look like bugs. Set up a relay race where kids must push the bugs to the finish line using only their noses.

## Craft Options

**Bug Hut**—Make pretend bug huts out of empty oatmeal containers. Turn them upside down, and cut out windows and doors. Paint or cover them with construction paper and decorate with bug illustrations. Hand out fake bugs to live in the huts.

**Cardboard Caterpillars**—Tear off the lids of cardboard egg cartons, then split the egg carton in half lengthwise. Turn it over and you have two caterpillars! Provide magic markers to decorate, use pipe cleaners for antennae, and glue on movable eyes.

**Bug Mobile**—Make bug mobiles on hangers. Hang magazine pictures of bugs by attaching pieces of yarn in varying lengths between the picture and the hanger.

## Food & Treat Selections

For whatever food you serve, make it fun by renaming it in a bug-related way. Remember, black shoestring licorice makes great bug legs on most food! A sample menu could include:

Ham'bug'ers in a Cocoon (hamburgers on a roll)
Grasshopper Legs in Mud (celery sticks in dip)
Ladybug Chunks (pieces of watermelon)
Fruit Fly Jumble (fruit salad)

Termite Treats (chocolate chip cookies)
Insect Juice and Honeybee Nectar (fruit punch and lemonade)

**Spider Sandwiches**—Spread peanut butter between two chocolate cookie wafers. Add chocolate shoestring licorice pieces for legs. Adhere chocolate chip "eyes" with frosting.

## Cake Possibilities

**Cupcake Caterpillar**—Line up a bunch of cupcakes to simulate a caterpillar. Place licorice antennae and candy eyes on the leading cupcake. Cut green Fruit Roll-ups into leaf shapes and place under and around the cupcakes.

**Dirt Dessert**—See recipe on page 9 and place gummy worms on top.

## Favors To Go

These party guests will be "itching" to take something home! Give them boxes of plastic bugs in small clear containers with lids. Include toy tweezers and a miniature magnifying glass.

Keep "bugging" the kids with other favors to go: packages of gummy worms, bug tattoos, fly swatters (kids love them!), or fly-in-the-ice-cube trick toys. You can find additional items in nature stores and gag gift stores.

# The Wetter the Better!

**For a wet and wild water party, have a pool party
without the pool! No reason for a rain date—
so what if it rains on the party?
All the more reason to get wet!**

## The Invitation

**Balloon**—Let the water battle begin! Prepare the guests for
a water balloon fight by writing party details with a marker on a
deflated balloon (blow it up to do so but do not tie). Instruct
them to blow up the balloon.

**Water Bottle**—For a hand delivered invitation, place invitations inside of empty water bottles (the kind with a straw and lid) or write the party details with marker on the outside of the water bottles. Tie deflated blue balloons with curly blue ribbon to the straw.

## What to Wear

Make sure that guests know they will get very soaked at this party! Tell them to wear swimsuits and bring a towel and change of clothes.

## Decoration Ideas

**Blue By You**—No pool of water at this celebration, but a blue decor will provide a cool, watery feeling! Decorate the table with a fish or beach theme tablecloth. Plenty of varying colors of blue balloons should adorn this outside party area. Table accessories can also be blue: cups, utensils, napkins, and plates.

**Water Fun**—Set up a kiddie pool and a water slide mat for more splashin' fun. Blow up rafts and inner tubes. Scatter around a bunch of pool toys.

## Games & Activities To Play and Do

**Sprinkler Fun**—Provide a few water sprinklers attached to garden hoses for children to run through. There's always a sprinkler craze on the market every summer. Check out toy stores for the latest one.

**Car Wash**—Let the kids wash the cars! Set out all the supplies ahead of time: several hoses, buckets, sponges, detergent, window cleaner and paper towels. They'll have a ball!

**Treasure Dig**—Half fill a large styrofoam cooler with sand. Bury small trinkets such as marbles, necklaces, plastic toys and wrapped candy. Let kids take turns digging for treasure. Time each dig at a minute, or limit the number of items each child is allowed to remove from the treasure chest. Provide small loot bags or toy treasure chests for their findings.

**Balloon People**—Cut out foot shapes from pieces of sturdy cardboard. Slide the knot of an inflated balloon into slits cut into the cardboard so that balloons stand up. Let kids decorate the balloons with shaving cream or whipped cream. Give each kid a heavy duty water pistol and have a race to see who can squirt off the cream first!

**Water Battles**—Provide water balloons, wet sponges and squirt guns for more wet fun! Encourage the children to be gentle with each other. Buy water guns for every kid and write names on them (these are take home favors).

**Water Bomb Pass**—Place the kids in a large circle. Poke a pinhole in a balloon filled with water and pass it around quickly. The object of the game is not to be the one holding the balloon when all the water has leaked out.

**Water Baseball**—Fill lots of water balloons, and use a plastic bat to play a game of water baseball.

**Wet Feet**—Kids sit on small chairs around a water-filled baby pool with their feet dangling in. On the count of 1-2-3-GO!, dump a bunch of floating toys (like rubber ducks and frogs) into the pool. Everyone tries to remove the toys with their feet.

**Water Relay**—Provide teams with small cups and two buckets (one full of water, one empty). Team members scoop up a cup of water from one bucket, run a few yards to the empty bucket, dump in the water, then return to the back of the line. The next team member does the same thing, then the next, etc. The winning team is the first who fills up the empty bucket with water. They then get to drench the losing team!

## Craft Options

**Umbrella Painting**—If it does rain on this party, the kids will be equipped with personalized umbrellas. Provide plain kids' umbrellas and fabric paint for each child to create a design.

**Soap on a Rope**—Let kids paint (use tempera) white bars of soap. (If they are old enough to handle a small knife, they can also make soap carvings.) An adult precuts holes in one end of the soap with a letter opener or ice pick. String pieces of twine through the holes, making a knot so they won't slip through, and tie the ends.

## Food & Treat Selections

Water related food is the way to go to feed these dripping kids. Keep them outside while they munch!

**Boat Bottoms**—Hollow out French dinner rolls to resemble boat bottoms. Fill with tuna salad, shrimp salad or rolled up lunch meat and cheese.

**Watermelon Boat**—Cut a watermelon in half lengthwise, scoop out the insides, and fill with fresh fruit, including pieces of the watermelon.

**Fish Delights**—Serve goldfish crackers and gummy fish in real fish bowls.

**Individual Parfaits**—Use cubed blue gelatin and whipped cream and serve in individual paper cups.

**Sandy Stuff**—Fill individual clear plastic cups with vanilla pudding. Add finely crushed graham crackers to look like sand. Garnish with a cocktail umbrella and gummy starfish.

**Cool H$_2$O**—Set out individual bottled water. Write each kid's name on a bottle. Provide a blue drink for another thirst-quenching option.

## Cake Possibility

Dive into this cake creation! Make a rectangular cake and decorate with blue icing to represent a swimming pool. Outline the edges with white or black. Add a rectangular cookie wafer to one end for the diving board. Stick in a very small plastic ladder on one side, and small plastic toy people as swimmers. Use Lifesavers candy for inner tubes.

## Favors To Go

Send the kids downstream with one or two ideas out of this bunch of water-related favors: water bottles or beach buckets filled with candy, water bottles or sun visors decorated with guest's name, snorkel masks and fins, squirt guns, child's umbrellas, beach balls, swim rings and tubes, pool toys, sunglasses.

# The Safari Club

**Follow the paw prints and hunt for big game
in this Safari Club! This theme party is ideal
to host in the picnic area on zoo grounds.
Lions and tigers and bears, oh my!**

## The Invitation

**Busy Box of Animals**—For a hand-delivered invitation, write the details of the party on separate paper animal shapes and place inside a small box of animal crackers. For instance, make a paper giraffe silhouette and write the time. The address can be written on a paper monkey silhouette. Write the birthday child's name and age on an elephant shape, and the date can be written on a zebra shape. Add a few animal crackers for a yummy effect! See template, page 174.

**Jungle Jeep**—Invite guests to frolic in the jungle, but first they'll need a jeep to ride through the thicket. Write party details on a jeep shape cut from tan card stock. Black movable

39

paper wheels can be added using brass fasteners. Use a rubber stamp to make paw prints around the border of the jeep.

## What To Wear

To get close to the animals, children have to blend in with the color of the jungle! Ask them to wear animal print shirts, khaki pants, rope belts, or shirts printed with an animal picture.

## Decoration Ideas

**Tablecloth**—Lots of animal prints on this safari, especially on the table. Cover it with a large piece of animal print fabric and scatter around plastic zoo animals. Or, make a pattern out of a sheet of stenciling plastic (found in craft stores near stencil supplies) to resemble a paw print. Stencil paw prints all over white butcher paper using a black crayon or marker.

**Jazzy Jeep**—If you have a Jeep, park it near the party entrance and fill it with large stuffed animals and potted plants. Make zebra stripes on the Jeep with white shaving cream.

**More Jungle**—In the party area, arrange large plants and stuffed safari animals all around. Pitch a small tent. Play rainforest music.

**Paw Prints**—Using the same paw print stencil created for the tablecloth, stencil animal footprints with black chalk on an outside area surface (sidewalk, driveway, floor of pavilion).

## Games & Activities To Play and Do

**Mascot Visit**—Have an animal mascot such as a lion, bear, or tiger visit the party. Ask a local college or high school to send their mascot for a half hour or so.

**Animal Display**—Invite a local nature organization to display a live animal program of small creatures such as owls, snakes, reptiles, and birds.

**What Animal Am I?**—Cut out magazine pictures of animals and glue onto index cards. Kids pick a card and imitate the animal's sound until the other kids guess what animal.

**Egg Hunt**—Before the party, make a batch of plastic eggs with the name of an animal written in marker on each egg. For instance, make a batch of "zebras," a batch of "leopards" and a batch of "tigers." Fill the eggs with animal crackers or candy and tape shut. Provide maps of the party area for the "safari hunters" to find the required eggs for their team. For instance, Team One (name them "The Canteens") must find all of the zebra eggs. Team Two ("The Whiskers") must find all of the leopard eggs, and Team Three ("The Hunters") must find all of the tiger eggs. The eggs are then divided among the kids to take home.

**Noah's Search**—Assign animal names to each child, using two of each animal. At the start of the game, everyone imitates their assigned animal's sound as they prowl around the area. Each kid has to find a partner who is making the same animal sound. Once they do, they sit down to indicate they are finished.

**Peanut Pitch**—Paint an elephant (does not have to be elaborate) on plywood, foam board or an artist's canvas (found in art and craft stores). Cut out a hole in the elephant's mouth. Provide peanuts in the shell and let the kids take turns trying to toss peanuts into the elephant's mouth.

**Monkey Connection**—Using the game "Barrel of Monkeys" see who can connect the most monkeys together in one minute.

# Craft Options

**Safari Jeeps**--Before the party, spray paint a few cardboard boxes white. Cut out the tops and bottoms. The kids can make the rest of the jeep with materials such as green plastic foliage, black paper plates for wheels and the steering wheel, aluminum pie plates for headlights, and thick black markers to make zebra stripes. Use the jeeps to go on the egg hunt as mentioned on page 41.

**Lion's Mane**—Prepare orange party plates ahead of time by punching holes around the perimeter of each plate. Out of sticky-back felt, cut out triangles, circles and whiskers for the lion's features. Provide gold, tan and brown yarn for the kids to thread through the holes to make the lion's mane. Thread through more than one time to get a thicker mane.

**Binoculars**—Tape or hot glue together two toilet tissue paper rolls. Decorate the "binoculars" with animal stickers. Make straps out of yarn so the kids can wear them around their necks.

**Safari Scene**—On white paper, draw a simple jeep and a safari scene such as trees, plants and a tent. Make enough copies for each guest. The kids color the scene and then glue on animal crackers to complete the picture.

**Paper Zoo**—Make paper bag animal masks or puppets. Provide crayons, glue, scissors, and yarn. For puppets, paper lunch bags are the perfect size. For masks, use paper grocery bags.

**Glue a Zoo**—Make collages of zoo animals on poster board. Provide glue, scissors, and animal-related magazine photos.

**Rope Belts**—Provide thin lengths of rope (belt size) and various beads for the guests to string and make rope belts.

## Food & Treat Selections

**Animal Cracker Fun!**—Dip animal crackers in whipped topping or icing for a roaring treat! You can also make miniature peanut butter and jelly sandwiches between two animal crackers.

**What Is It?**—Rename the food with animal names such as Ostrich Burger, Endangered Hot Dog, Panther Pizza, and Tiger Tails (cover cheese curls with chocolate icing stripes). Frozen chocolate covered bananas on a popsicle stick can be called Monkey Arms.

**Jungle Fizz**— In a blender, puree' various pieces of fruit with ice for a refreshing fruit slushie. Just the thing to cool off after a hot safari ride!

## Cake Possibilities

**Zebra Cake**—Decorate any shaped cake in white icing. Add black jagged stripes to simulate a zebra. Adorn with a miniature toy jeep.

**Tiger Cake**—You can also decorate a cake to look like the head of a tiger. Use orange icing for the base color. With black icing, make tiger stripes across the cake. Use black shoestring licorice for whiskers and chocolate cookie wafers for the eyes.

## Favors To Go

Pack up the tents and jeep—this safari expedition is over! Here are a few ideas for kids to continue their safari fun at home: fill pith helmets or animal masks (sold at zoos and nature stores) with rubber snakes, plastic animals, animal noses, squirt guns, toy canteens, boxes of animal crackers, zoo passes, or zoo membership applications and brochures. Check the zoo's gift shop for more animal-related favors.

# Glowin' in the Dark

**No need for candles at this outside, evening party!
It glows enough to light up any birthday celebration!**

## The Invitation

Guests can't read this invitation unless they're in the dark! This glow-in-the-dark invitation is made out of black squares of foam sheets. Write "Glow-in-the-Dark Party for [child's name]" with a glow paint stick. Glue on a few glow-in-the-dark stars. Glue the foam square onto the cover of a folded piece of neon colored poster board or card stock, then write the party details inside with a black marker. Or, you can use black poster board or construction paper and write the details with a white marker.

**Envelopes**—Make homemade envelopes with black construction paper or visit an office supply store for a selection of envelopes. If you mail the invitation in a black envelope, use a large white mailing label so the post office can read the address.

## What to Wear

Kids will be heard and not seen at this party! Invite them to wear all black clothing, and any glow-in-the-dark shirts, shoes and accessories they may have. Light up the kids with glow necklaces and glow sticks so you can find them when it's time to cut the cake! You can also use reflective tape on their clothing.

## Decoration Ideas

**Everything Glows!**—Replace outside light bulbs with "black" light bulbs. Kids will get a charge out of seeing their teeth, fingernails, and clothes glow!

**Night Torches**—Safely place stick torches in the ground to light up the party area. Fill with citronella oil to keep the bugs away.

**Light Up**—Use white holiday lights to light up the deck and a few trees in the yard.

**Dark Decor**—Adorn the party area with black balloons and a black tablecloth and accessories. Cut out large white stars out of foam sheets to use as placemats and to add some contrast to the table. You can also place glow-in-the-dark stars on a plastic black tablecloth (no need to glue them).

## Games & Activities To Play and Do

**Star Discovery**—Set up a telescope and let kids take turns finding stars. Each kid selects his own star and names it. Give out stars cut from metallic paper and write the newly discovered star's name on them with a black marker.

**Lightning Bug Hunt**—Save plastic peanut butter jars and punch holes in the lids to hold lightning bugs. The kid who finds the most bugs wins a glow-in-the-dark prize. Release the bugs after the game.

**Star Gaze**—Lay a few blankets on the grass to star watch. See who can first spot a shooting star and then everyone makes a wish!

**Flashlight Tag**—Don't get caught by the beam of the light or you are "it!" Provide each kid with a cheap flashlight (check the dollar store) for this game.

**Under the Stars**—One option for this party is to hold a sleepover. Set up a few tents in the yard, or if they want, let the kids sleep under the stars. Whether you will join them or not is your call!

**Fireworks Show**—A nice touch to this glowing party is a small fireworks show. This should be handled only by adults and used only in states where fireworks are legal. Or, provide sparklers to light.

**The Black Hole**—Use a large plastic container with a lid (like a gallon ice cream bucket or giant size margarine container) and fill it with small items such as a comb, doll, marble, battery, troll, ball, etc. Cover the container in black construction paper. Cut a hole in the top of the lid, big enough for little hands to fit in. Taking turns, instruct each kid to find a specific item in The Black Hole. Replace the item after each turn.

**Ball Games**—Use an illuminated or glow-in-the-dark ball to play games such as SPUD, Kickball, or Dodgeball. Illuminated balls and glow-in-the-dark "moon balls" can be found in toy and craft stores.

**Pin the Cheese on the Moon**—Play this (blindfolded, of course—it will be dark anyway!) in the same way as Pin the Tail on the Donkey. Use a felt board and pieces of felt to make the moon and the cheese.

"Moon" Bounce—Use a trampoline or rent a moonbounce. Place either of these in a well lit area of the yard to prevent boo-boos. Follow safety rules.

# Craft Options

Paper Vests—Make vests out of brown grocery bags and decorate them with reflective tape. Kids can wear them during the party. This will make it much easier to spot them!

Glow Shirts—Decorate black plain T-shirts with glow-in-the-dark paint sticks. Have kids create their own galaxy or planet. These can be take home favors, but make the shirts early on in the party to give them a chance to dry.

Star Necklaces—Decorate precut foam stars and moons with glow-in-the-dark paint. Hole punch and add a piece of nylon string to each. Make necklaces, or hang them from trees in the yard.

# Food & Treat Selections

No glow-in-the-dark food at this party, but you can serve dark-colored food and food which imitates things that glow.

Moon Rolls—Make ham and cheese or tuna salad sandwiches on "crescent" rolls (simulates the moon). Put a few black olives on decorative toothpicks and stick in the top of the sandwiches.

Moon Cheese—Serve Swiss cheese (like the moon's surface) on round crackers.

Galaxy Gelatin—Serve blackberry gelatin with whipped topping and star sprinkles on top.

Tasty Treats—star-shaped cookies, black licorice, dark chocolate brownies with star sprinkles, raisins.

## Cake Possibility

Make a devil's food cake and cover it in dark chocolate or dark blue icing to simulate the evening sky. Draw lots of stars with white or yellow icing and use edible glitter. Use sparklers instead of candles to really illuminate this cake!

## Favors To Go

Make the guests "glow" with delight when they find these goodies in black paper bags with yellow star stickers: glow in the dark stars and moons, glow-sticks, flashlights, laser swords, mini telescopes, kaleidoscopes, glow-in-the-dark paint sticks, reflective bike stickers, glow-in-the-dark bugs, sparklers. A nature store may have more night-time related ideas.

# USA Olympics

*Calling all athletes!*
*It's time for an Olympic competition to show everyone*
*who is number one! On your mark, get set, GO!*

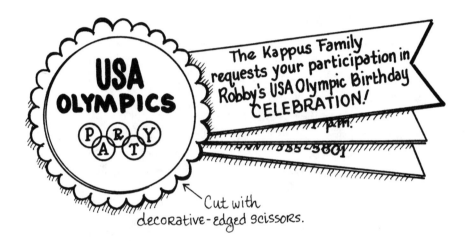

Cut with decorative-edged scissors.

## The Invitation

**Award Ribbon**—Stand up proud, America! Write party details on three pieces (one red, one white, one blue) of wide ribbon attached to a round piece of construction paper to simulate an award ribbon. Use a fine tip black marker or black ballpoint pen to write party info. USA OLYMPICS PARTY can be written on the round part.

**Fancy Flag**—Use red, white and blue ribbon to tie an invitation to the stick of a small American flag.

## What to Wear

**Kids**—Some vigorous activity will be happening at this party. Invite guests to wear sneakers and red, white and blue athletic clothing such as warm-up suits, T-shirts, shorts, and sweatpants.

**Adults**—Parents can wear black and white striped "referee" shirts, whistles around their necks, and carry clipboards.

## Decoration Ideas

**Three Colors**—It's red, white and blue all the way! Hang a large American flag outside. Put up lots of 4th of July decorations. Bunches of red, white and blue balloons can be tethered to outside furniture, deck and trees.

**Winner's Stand**—Make a three-tiered winner's platform out of square plastic crates (three on the bottom level, then two, then one on the top). Secure them together with wire. Make a #1 sign for the top position, a #2 sign for the middle, and a #3 sign for the bottom crates. Test the crate structure before using to make sure it is sturdy enough.

**Thirst Quenchers**—Set out three large containers of drinks and small paper cups, like in a sporting event. Have red punch in one, lemonade in another, and a blue drink in the third.

**Racing Lanes**—Make relay racing lanes with lime (cut hole in corner and pour from bag), or spray paint lines on the grass. Make a 'START' and 'FINISH' line.

**Posters**—Make a large poster depicting the five Olympic rings. For each activity and game station, make a poster board sign on a stick.

## Games & Activities To Play & Do

**Opening Ceremony**—Every Olympic event has an opening ceremony. No exception here! Use a small yard torch to lead the line of kids around the yard while inspiring and upbeat music is played from a tape or cd.

**Team Time**—Organize party guests in teams for each activity. Use a cap gun or pop a balloon to start each race. Here are a few activity ideas:

| | |
|---|---|
| baton pass | gymnastics mat for tumbling |
| running race | twirling long ribbon on a stick |
| trampoline jumping | weight lifting (use hand weights) |
| frisbee throw | basketball shoot |
| pillowcase hop | people wheelbarrow race |
| egg on a spoon relay | hula hoop contest |

**Closing Ceremony**—Organize an awards ceremony to hold after the games. Let groups of three stand on the winner's platform. Award them with gold medals on ribbons to put around their necks. Take pictures with an instant camera for take home favors.

## Craft Option

Stars and Stripes Forever!—This American flag is made out of woven construction paper. Provide whole sheets of red construction paper for each kid, with vertical slits cut in the paper. Cut white stripes of paper (about ½") and weave these through the slits. Add a square of blue construction paper in the left corner and apply 50 white star stickers. These are flags the children will be proud of!

## Food & Treat Selections

This event calls for basic cookout food. Think 4th of July! Serve hamburgers and hot dogs on rolls, cold salads such as potato salad and coleslaw, pickles, olives, potato chips and dip, red/white/blue snowballs, and of course, good old American apple pie!

## Cake Possibility

**Edible American Flag**—Make a pound cake in a rectangular pan. Cover it entirely with whipped topping. Line up rows of 50 blueberries in the corner for the stars, and line up halved strawberries across the cake for the stripes.

**Luscious Logo**—Decorate an oblong cake with white icing and draw on the Olympic logo (five intertwined rings, each a different color).

## Favors To Go

Everyone is a winner when they take home a few Olympic related party favors. Include whistles on a string, stopwatches, awards ribbons, and miniature American flags. Place in small red bags with handles and apply blue and white star stickers.

# Fashion Folly

**Pretty as a Picture is how these girls will look before leaving this party! Dress up these fashion models, apply lipstick, and set up the lights and camera!**

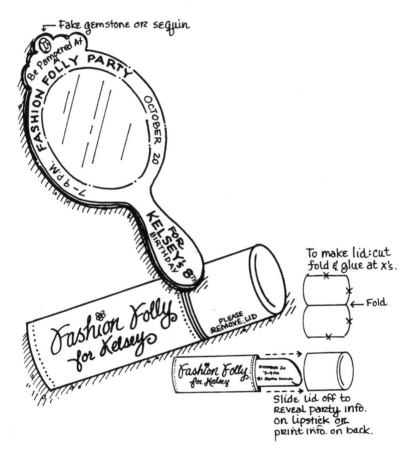

Fake gemstone or sequin

Be Pampered At
FASHION FOLLY PARTY
OCTOBER 20
7-9 P.M.
FOR KELSEY'S 8 BIRTHDAY

*Fashion Folly for Kelsey*

PLEASE REMOVE LID

To make lid: cut fold & glue at x's.
← Fold

*Fashion Folly for Kelsey*

Slide lid off to reveal party info. on lipstick or print info. on back.

## The Invitation

**Handheld Mirror**—The girls will see how pretty they are already by looking at this invitation. Glue an oval piece of silver wrapping paper or aluminum foil onto a bright pink mirror made of foam board. Write party details around the handle perimeter or on the back. See template on page 175. When parents RSVP, ask them if it is okay for their daughter to have her hair done, makeup applied, and nails painted.

**Lipstick Tube**—Make a mock lipstick tube out of red or pink construction paper. The cap is simply a separate piece of construction paper which slides off to announce the party details. Decorate with rubber stamp lips or apply red lipstick on your child's lips and let her kiss each invitation. See template, page 176.

## What to Wear

Their fashionable attire will make these guests even more lovely! Ask them to dress up for the occasion in their trendiest clothes.

## Decorations

**Posters and Photos**—Let the girls "model" themselves after fashion model photos from magazines which are hung around the room. Hang up posters of your guests' favorite movie stars, models and rock stars.

**Face of a Model**—Secure a poster of a fashion model on a large piece of foam board and cut out the face. Let kids stand behind it and put their faces in the hole. Take instant pictures for take home favors.

**Pretty Placemats**—Make placemats out of fashion magazine covers. Adhere to cardboard and cover with clear contact paper or have them laminated at a copy center or office supply store.

## Games & Activities To Play and Do

**Dress-ups**—Provide a box full of clothes and accessories so that everyone can "dress up." Before the party, visit yard sales, scan your closet and ask your friends for a collection of used clothing. Be sure there is enough in the box for everyone to try on a few pieces: dresses, hats, purses, shoes, jewelry, scarves, gloves. After the party, give away the dress-up box to a charity or preschool, or give it to your daughter as a birthday gift.

**Make-up Madness**—Let the girls experiment with makeup, or ask a mom to apply their makeup. Supply wipes, tissue, and mirrors. Again, make sure you have parents' permission before applying makeup on the girls.

**Hair Braiding**—Invite a hair stylist friend to style or braid hair. With parental permission, the girls can have their hair washed, cut and blow-dried.

**Nails and Designs**—Ask a friend, babysitter or professional to do manicures, nail designs and pedicures. Set up a few small fans to help dry the polish quickly.

**Photo Shoot**—Set up an area in the party room for a photo shoot. Hang a light colored bed sheet and set up a pretty chair or stool in front of it. After each girl's hair, nails and makeup are finished, snap lots of pretend shots as if you are the photographer and she is the model. Then take one real snapshot with an instant camera for a take-home favor.

## Craft Options

**Jewelry Making**—Provide beads and colorful cord to make earrings, necklaces, rings, and bracelets. If you buy ready-made craft kits, make sure they have enough materials for every party guest.

**Decorative Brush & Comb Set**—Provide puffy paint, plain brushes and combs. Girls can decorate the handles with their names, flowers, lips, hearts, butterflies, and doodles.

## Food and Treat Selections

Whatever food you make for this party, make it very "pretty!" The girls will feel quite lovely as they are served luscious treats such as petit fours, finger sandwiches, and pinwheels (peanut butter and jelly roll-ups or olives and cream cheese). Serve iced tea with sugar cubes. Serve pretty cookies as a treat.

## Cake Possibility

Cut a rectangular cake into the shape of a lipstick tube and decorate it with colorful sprinkles. Color one end of the cake pink or red to simulate the cap of the lipstick tube. Or, with icing, draw a tube of lipstick on top of the cake.

## Favors To Go

This photo shoot is over! Send these pretty party guests on their way to be discovered with a stock of ladylike accessories. Place a few of these in small cosmetic bags or colorful plastic boxes: candy lips, costume jewelry, nail polish, perfume, hair accessories, combs, brushes, purse mirrors, candy necklaces, lip gloss or flavored lip balm. Ask a local department store or a makeup rep for perfume samples and lipsticks.

# The Construction Zone

**Yield to this construction sight as kids bulldoze their way right through this party! A few hours of creative construction will definitely yield tired little workers!**

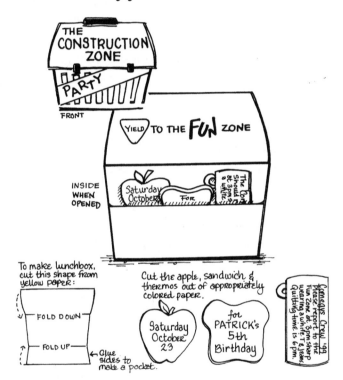

THE CONSTRUCTION ZONE

PARTY

FRONT

YIELD TO THE FUN ZONE

INSIDE WHEN OPENED

Saturday October

For

The Co should at 3 pm a white

To make lunchbox, cut this shape from yellow paper:

FOLD DOWN

FOLD UP

← Glue sides to make a pocket.

Cut the apple, sandwich & thermos out of appropriately colored paper.

Saturday October 23

for PATRICK's 5th Birthday

Conreays Crew '91 Please report to the Fun Zone at 3 pm sharp wearing a white T & jeans. Quitting time is 6 pm.

## The Invitation

**Lunchbox Lift**—Make a lunchbox out of yellow construction paper, making a flap to be lifted. The party details are included on separate paper shapes and inserted in lunchbox. See templates, pages 177 and 178.

STOP!—Little party guests will certainly stop to read this invitation! Look around for small versions of "yield" or "stop" signs (sold as car window stick-ups with suction cups) and write the party details on the back.

## What to Wear

Invite kids to blend into this construction sight as they wear yellow and black clothes. Or, make them look like miniature construction workers as they wear jeans, white T-shirts, and work boots. Provide clear safety glasses, carpenter aprons, orange safety vests, and hardhats. These items can be sent home as party favors in small cream colored canvas bags to simulate tool bags (check craft stores).

## Decoration Ideas

**Sign Sayings**—Make signs which read "Party Under Construction," "Party Zone," and "Construction Ahead." Make road signs such as STOP and YIELD out of red and yellow poster board, or borrow real ones from a local road repair facility.

**Horses and Cones**—Set up saw horses and small orange cones leading the way into the party, or set up inside for games. Use yellow crepe paper to simulate "caution" tape (or buy this at a hardware store) and string it between the cones. You can also use two saw horses and a piece of plywood (secured) for a makeshift table.

**Toy Box**—Set out toy tools, small boards to build with, real tool bags and tool boxes (real tools not recommended.) Set out cardboard blocks that resemble bricks.

**Balloons**—Decorate with orange, yellow, and black balloons.

**Placemats**—Make STOP and YIELD signs out of foam sheets.

## Games & Activities To Play and Do

**Sandbox Skills**— Let the kids have free play in a sandbox filled with toy trucks, cranes, shovels, buckets, and containers.

**A Cool House**—Build a house out of a refrigerator box. Provide markers, crayons, and scissors and let the little workers construct.

Cut away top portion of box for a roof.

**Keep On Truckin'**— Ask a builder or construction company to bring by one of their dump trucks, cement trucks, cranes or another construction vehicle for the kids to see up close. The driver can explain how the vehicle operates, and perhaps let the kids climb safely into the cab.

**Nail It**—Using pegs and a peg board, teach the proper and safe way to hammer nails.

**Creative Construction**—Set out blocks, logs, Legos, erector sets, and other building toys for kids to "construct."

**Obstacle Course**—While pulling a wagon containing a bucket of water, kids have to maneuver through orange cones without spilling the water.

**Brick Pile**—Using cardboard blocks that resemble bricks, pile them higher and higher and let the kids jump over at each height (like reverse limbo). Provide a cushion for them to land on.

## Craft Options

**Designer Lunchboxes**—Decorate plain kids' lunchboxes with stickers and markers.

**Paper Construction**—Provide large sheets of white butcher paper, marbles, acrylic paints, and small paper cups. Put a different color of paint in each cup and drop in a marble. Remove the marble from the cup and roll it around on the paper, which is being held between two people. The kids can pretend their marble is a "wrecking ball." The ball will create a design as it rolls around. Use various colors on the same sheet of paper. You can also place the paper inside of a large box lid to make it easier to roll the marble.

**Miniature Houses**—Build small houses using pint size milk cartons as the base. Use peanut butter for "cement," and use graham cracker squares for the walls and roof. Garnish with candy and mini cheese crackers, or cover the entire house with pretzel sticks to simulate log cabins.

## Food and Treat Selections

**What's for lunch?**—Open the lunchboxes to see! Include sandwiches in plastic bags, small bags of chips, pieces of fruit and thermos' full of lemonade, just like on the job!

**Stop Light Cookies**—Use a sugar cookie recipe to make rectangular shaped cookies. Line up one red, yellow and green m&m on each cookie before baking.

## Cake Possibilities

**Brick Wall Cake**—Make a rectangular cake and decorate it with red and black icing to resemble a brick wall. Stick in a trowel.

**Dump Truck Cake**—With icing, draw a simple shape of a dump truck. "Load" the back of the dump truck with candy. Use chocolate covered donuts for the wheels.

**Road Cake**—Decorate a sheet cake like a road using crushed chocolate cookies to simulate asphalt. Use white icing for road lines and green icing for grass. Garnish the highway with small toy construction vehicles.

## Favors To Go

It's quitting time—this work day is over! Send the tired construction workers home with plastic yellow lunchboxes filled with candy goodies, toy trucks, construction vehicles or building toys such as Lincoln Logs, Legos or blocks.

Or, roll orange cones from poster board and fill them with goodies or candy. Wrap the tops in clear plastic so the contents stay inside.

Or, see WHAT to WEAR for the tool bag idea.

# The Happy Camper

Pitch the tents and light a campfire! You have just
become a Camp Counselor for the night. A megaphone
and a whistle is highly recommended to help guide these
happy campers through an active campout encounter!

HELLO
HAPPY CAMPER!
You're Invited to
Pitch a Tent @
CAMP DANTE

May 15
7pm til 9 am.

RSVP to
Camp Counselor Suzanne @
555-ANGL

Deliver with trail mix
attached (left). Or, Roll up
& tie with something
earthy like Raffia or a
clover stem (below).

## The Invitation

Hello Happy Campers—Entice the guests with a flyer to attend this overnight campout. Name the camp after the child (i.e.,
"Camp Dante") and ask guests to make a camp reservation by
calling the Camp Counselor (you). Use camping-related art such
as a tent or campfire on the flyer and throughout the party
decor (on banner, signs, T-shirts, favor bags, etc.). See template,
page 179.

Trail Mix—Staple campout flyers on the outside of plastic
sandwich bags full of homemade trail mix: peanuts, raisins, dried
fruit, chocolate chips, peanut butter chips, m&m's, and cereal.
These will have to be hand delivered.

# What to Wear

**Kids**—In addition to bringing their sleeping bags and pillows, the guests' camping gear will include shorts, hiking boots, and hats. Hand out printed T-shirts with the camp logo that read "Camp Dante, May 15th" (use birthday child's name and date of party).

**Adults**—Hosting parents can wear badges which read "Camp Director." Provide "Counselor" badges for adult volunteers. Give the adults whistles to wear on cords around their necks. (These may be needed depending on how many kids are invited!)

# Decoration Ideas

**Tent Site**—Set up a group of tents in the yard, or rent a few tent sites at a campground. Provide enough sleeping space for everyone. (Note: this party does not have to be a sleep-over. If it is an overnighter, borrow a few friends to help with the event.)

**Big Banner**—Hang a "Welcome to Camp Dante" (again, use birthday child's name) banner in front of the house, around the tent area or between two trees. Lead the way with "Camp Dante" signs leading into the neighborhood.

**Listen Up!**—Give directions to the kids by speaking into a megaphone.

**Fire Circle**—Make a safe fire circle surrounded with rocks. Around the campfire area, set up a few bales of hay on which to sit. Check local ordinances about having a campfire at your residence.

# Games & Activities To Play and Do

**Scavenger Hunt**—Make up a list of things to find in nature such as a yellow leaf, a stick with three prongs, a bug, a flat rock, etc. Divide the group into a few teams so they can work together.

**Storytelling**—Tell a favorite scary story or let the kids take turns telling theirs. Or, read a ghost story from a library book. You can also begin a made-up scary story with a few sentences, then let each kid add on to the story as it travels around the circle. It will be interesting to hear the details and the ending of their adventure!

**Campfire Songs**—Sing around the campfire. Check library or scout books for classic kids' songs that everyone may recognize.

**Lights Out**—Establish a time for bedtime and flashlights out. Give the kids about 20 minutes to settle down inside their tents before you call "All Quiet." Make sure to tell them that they will have to hunt for their breakfast in the morning. (See Food.)

**Water Fun**—Provide every guest with a squirt gun and have a water battle! Depending on the size of the water guns you select, and the temperature of the evening, you may want to provide rain ponchos.

**Flashlight Tag**—This is like the regular game of tag, except that the person who is "it" uses the beam of a flashlight to make a "tag."

## Craft Options

**Totem Pole**—Provide thin, long pieces of wood, crayons and markers. Kids decorate the wood with designs and markings to resemble totem poles.

**Hat Painting**—Paint plain painter's caps (available in craft stores). Provide fabric markers or puffy paint.

**Nature Craft**—Glue alphabet soup letters to small rocks or thin pieces of bark. Spell out the guest's name, the date and the camp name.

**Stone Creatures**—Glue felt features such as ears, a nose and a mouth onto smooth stones. Add wiggly eyes.

**Fire Starters**—Collect dryer lint and cardboard egg cartons before the party. Stuff dryer lint into each hole of the egg cartons. Pour melted wax over the lint. Let cool. Break up egg cartons into sections. These fire starters work very well! Try them out with the kids when you light the campfire.

**Nature Frame**—Make picture frames out of nature objects by gluing pine cones, small stones and sticks around the border of clear, acrylic frames. Take instant pictures of the group and put one in every frame.

## Food & Treat Selections

**Burgers and Dogs**—Over the fire, roast hot dogs on a stick and cook hamburgers on a grate.

**Raw Eggs on Toast**—Tell the kids early on that you are going to make them eat "raw eggs on toast" before they go to bed. Serve slices of pound cake with a dollop of whipped cream. Add canned peach halves on top. This resembles a raw egg on toast!

**Mmmmmmmarshmallows!**—Roast marshmallows on sticks or make s'mores over the fire (melt thin chocolate bars and marsh-mallows between two graham crackers.) Provide clean sticks for roasting or buy metal sticks sold in a camping store.

**Jungle Breakfast**—In the morning, organize a "jungle break-fast." Be sure to tell them the night before that they will have to "hunt" for their breakfast. In the morning, while the kids are still asleep, hang lunch bags from trees (if you can) or hide them around the area. The bags will be filled with pieces of fruit, mini cereal boxes, juice boxes and toaster pastries or donuts.

## Cake Possibilities

**Camp Cake**—Give the bakery a picture of the camp logo to transfer it onto the cake, or draw it yourself with icing. Or, write "Camp Dante" (use your child's name) with icing and draw simple camp-related artwork such as a tent and campfire.

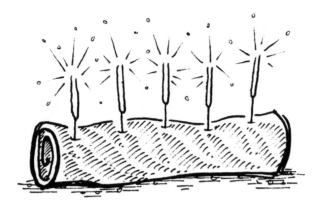

Log Roll—Make a batch of brownies, but bake them on a cookie sheet so they will be thin. Spread the brownie batter to all ends and sides of the cookie sheet. While the sheet of brownies is still warm, roll it so that it becomes a log shape. Use sparklers for candles.

## Favors To Go

This camping trip is over! Make sure you have happy campers as you hand out this bag of goodies: glow in the dark bugs, rubber snakes, nesting utensils and cups, rain ponchos, and water guns. Place the favors in brown paper lunch bags with the camp logo, and tie them closed with twine. Include thank you notes on the outside of the bag with your child's signature.

# You're The Star, Hollywood!

**The stars are out and we don't mean the ones
in the sky! A classy night is in store for party guests
as they fly to Hollywood for their big chance to shine in
the spotlight. Hurray for Hollywood!**

## The Invitation

**Hollywood Head Shot**—"Excuse me, but my agent is calling!"
Send an instant picture of head shots of the birthday girl
dressed all "Hollywood:" evening gown, feather boa, white gloves,
sunglasses, and bold jewelry. Insert the photos into blank greeting
cards which have
slots or fold a piece
of card stock and
glue it on the front.
Decorate the border
with rhinestones, glitter,
fake gems, star
stickers, or a star
rubber stamp.

**Cover Girl**—Create
a magazine cover
on the computer and
place your child's
photo in the center
as the "Cover Girl."
Party details can be
written on it like
"teasers" on an actual
magazine cover.
Enclose star confetti
in the envelope.

67

## What to Wear

Get everyone ready for the paparazzi as you ask the children to dress like they are attending the "Oscars." Boys can wear suits; girls can wear long dresses, hats, gloves, and jewelry. Or, the kids can dress up like their favorite movie stars.

## Decoration Ideas

**Starry Sidewalk**—These guests will feel like they are in Hollywood, California when they see the stars on the sidewalk, just like in front of Gromin's Chinese Theater. Draw large stars on the sidewalk with chalk and write in the guests' names, then outline your child's hand on each star.

**Hollywood's Big**—They'll see these a mile away, just like the ones on the hill! Make large letters spelling out the word HOLLYWOOD out of white foam board or styrofoam. Place near the party entrance, or in the foyer.

**A Star is Born**—Decorate the front door with a large star reading "Angelica's Dressing Room" (use your child's name). Shine a few spotlights on the front door to illuminate it.

**Musical Melodies**—Play the "Hurray for Hollywood" tune and other Broadway show tunes on a tape or cd player.

**Ceiling Scenery**—Hang lots of stars from the ceiling and tape them to the walls around the party area.

**Posters and Signs**—Hang up movie posters. Ask local theaters or video stores for extras. Make signs which read QUIET ON THE SET and ON THE AIR.

**Just for Fun**—Include a director's chair and a megaphone. Set up cameras and video cameras on tripods.

**Dressing Room**—Set up a "dressing room" area. Use a child's playset vanity with lights. Set out lotion, makeup, brush and comb, perfume, mints, and toiletries.

**So Elegant**—Set an "elegant" table using gold or silver paperware and plastic champagne flutes. Use real cloth napkins or cut-up pieces of fabric. Make gold star-shaped placemats out of foam sheets or construction paper covered with clear contact paper (or laminate).

**Live TV!**—Decorate the front of the TV with a large photo of your child to simulate an appearance on television.

## Games & Activities To Play and Do

**Lights! Camera! Action!**—Prepare an easy script of a well-known TV show or movie. Prepare the props ahead of time. Let the kids act it out while you videotape it, and then let them watch it later. Make sure each guest has a role in the production unless she chooses not to participate. A parent can narrate.

**Product Promo**—Let the kids create their own commercials on videotape by making up silly products to promote.

**Oscar Night**—Pretend the guests are all receiving "Oscars." Use a toy microphone to introduce each person and announce what award category they have won. Make it silly, like Best Actress in the movie, "I Don't Wanna Go To Bed," Best Supporting Actress in "Don't Make Me Go To School," and Best Director for "Do I Have To Eat My Broccoli?" Videotape each guest making a speech and hamming it up! Later, make and send copies of the videotape to the kids.

**Great Games**—Have relay races in high heels . . . have races where partners apply makeup to each other in a limited time . . . do karaoke . . . play charades using only TV stars and shows, and movies and movie stars . . . play "Hollywood Squares" using the board game or make up your own . . . have a trivia contest using details from cartoons and kids' TV shows.

**On With the Show**—Have a few volunteer moms apply makeup. Organize a fashion show, providing the clothes to model, or arrange a silly talent show.

## Craft Options

**Handprints**—Make each guest's handprint in a plaster star. Let them carve in their name. Craft stores carry the kits to make this craft.

**Stars**—Decorate "dressing room" stars with glitter and sequins and write the kids' names on them.

## Food & Treat Selections

You'll be the star of the show when you serve these yummy treats to your talented guests!

- peanut butter and jelly sandwiches cut into star shapes (use a cookie cutter)
- star shaped sugar cookies
- fake caviar (blackberry gelatin cut up in very small pieces)
- star shaped Rice Krispie treats (use a cookie cutter while they are still warm) or gelatin pieces
- popcorn
- ginger ale with strawberries floating in plastic champagne flutes

## Cake Possibilities

**Star Cake**—Either cut a star shape out of a round cake or draw a star with edible glitter.

**Hollywood Cake**—Write HOLLYWOOD across a large sheet cake.

**Take One**—Draw a "scene slapper" on a cake.

## Favors To Go

Fade out this star-studded evening and send the actors and actresses back to their dressing rooms with a few of these favors: sunglasses, fake "Oscars" (check in a party store for statues), feather boas, tiaras, toy cameras or throw-away cameras, movie passes, movie candy and popcorn. Put favors inside plastic black top hats or theater popcorn bags.

# Boot Camp

**Left Right, 1-2, Left Right, 3-4, Left Right, 1-2-3-4, 1-2-3-4!! This is the cadence for a boot camp party as the kids are camouflaged and ready for action. March onward!**

Glue at all outer edges except at top.

Uncle Sam wants **YOU** to join the fun at Bradley's Boot Camp Birthday Party...
Saturday, September 12
12 - 3 p.m.
RSVP - Becky 555-1234

## The Invitation

These boots are made for walking! Make two boot shapes out of black construction paper to look like an army boot. Glue the two boots together at the borders. Print the party details on a separate piece of paper and slip it in between, as if you were placing the invitation inside of the boot. Punch holes for the shoestring, and lace it up using a piece of real shoestring. See template, page 180.

## What to Wear

Sir, Yes, Sir! These kids will pay closer attention to their drill sergeant when they are dressed like army personnel: camouflage or army green T-shirt, khaki pants, and hiking boots or high-top black boots. Or, the kids can dress in all green and brown clothing.

**Face Paint**—Paint their faces a mixture of brown and green to "camouflage" them.

**Name Tags**—Make name tags for the kids to wear which read "PFC Singleton" (use last names). Adults can wear name tags which read "General" and "Lieutenant." Use the kind of name tags which are enclosed in plastic and have pins on the back.

## Decoration Ideas

**Mess Hall**—It's a regulation mess hall with an all brown and green color scheme. Use a piece of camouflage fabric as a tablecloth. Make black boots for placemats out of black construction paper. Cover the party area with camouflage material—drape it, hang it, and place it around the perimeter of the room.

**More Decor**—Set out an inflatable boat with oars. Decorate the party area using dark green balloons.

## Games & Activities To Play and Do

**Obstacle Course**—Set up an obstacle course in the yard such as the following: run in and out of a group of trees, climb on each piece of a swingset (down the slide, hang on the bar, jump over a swing), climb over a short wall or hedge, jump over buckets of water, climb over a fence, run around the picnic table twice.

**Raft Race**—Set up a kiddie pool. Kids race their boats (see craft) by blowing them across the water.

**Stone Face**—In the army, boot camp personnel are not allowed to crack a smile or show expression, especially when a superior is speaking to them. In this game, one person must keep a straight face while another tries to make him laugh.

**Hot Grenade**—Fill up a dark green balloon with water. Prick a pin hole in the balloon so it creates a small leak. Kids quickly pass around the balloon while standing in a circle, acting as if it is a "hot grenade." The object is not to be the one holding the balloon when it is empty.

**Warhead Contest**—Hand out a piece of "Warhead" candy to each guest. Kids suck the candy while trying not to make a face (this candy is very sour!). The winner is the kid who does not crack an expression while eating the candy.

**Sergeant, May I?**—Most kids know how to play the game, Mother, May I. Change the game to Sergeant, May I. One person is chosen to be the drill sergeant and stands at one end of the yard. He gives "commands" to his troop one at a time as they are lined up at the other end of the yard. For instance, the drill sergeant tells Emma, "Take four marching steps." Emma then has to ask, "Sergeant, May I?" before obeying the command. The drill sergeant then moves onto the next kid, "Sammy, do two stomach crawls." Sammy has to ask, "Sergeant, May I?", do two stomach crawls, and so on. If a child fails to ask "Sergeant, May I?," he has to go back to the starting line. The first kid who reaches the drill sergeant is the winner.

**G.I. Joe Says**—You can also play "Simon Says" switching the format like the game above. Use different military tactics like salute, at ease, karate chop, etc.

**Free Play**—Set out army men, toy tanks, jeeps, army trucks, and other army-related toys for the children to play with at their leisure.

## Craft Options

**Styrofoam Rafts**—Make rafts out of styrofoam meat trays and straws. The meat tray is the base of the raft. Glue straws side by side to simulate bamboo lined up. Make sails on the rafts using straws and pieces of paper. Race the rafts (see Games).

**Army Jeeps**—Before the party, spray paint a few cardboard boxes camouflage (available in hardware stores). Cut out the tops and bottoms. The kids can make the rest of the jeep with materials such as green plastic foliage, black paper plates for wheels and the steering wheel, and aluminum pie plates for headlights.

**Binoculars**—Tape or hot glue together two toilet tissue paper rolls. Make straps out of yarn. Decorate the rolls using markers and crayons.

## Food & Treat Selections

**Rations**—Let kids make their own "rations" bag. Provide individual bowls of peanuts, m&m's, raisins, cereal, banana chips, chocolate chips, peanut butter chips, dried fruit, and granola. Place in green lunch bags.

**Trays and Kits**—If you are serving lunch, use plastic cafeteria trays to simulate a mess hall. Serve the food in mess kits, then send these home as a party favor.

## Cake Possibility

Decorate a cake with green icing. Draw the outline of a black combat boot. Use black shoestring licorice for the shoestrings.

## Favors To Go

Place a few of these inside of toy army helmets: squirt guns, canteens, dog tags, army figures, army action dolls, toy binoculars. Wrap in brown or green mesh.

Other favor ideas: mess kits, collapsible cups, plastic utensils hooked together. Check out army surplus and camping stores for more related accessories.

# Afternoon Teddy-Bear Tea

*Little girls will feel all grown up sharing afternoon tea with their friends, just like Mommy! Their teddy bear "dates" provide a familiar friend and added fun.*

## The Invitation

Teddys and tea set the mood for this special occasion. Cut two tea cup shapes from construction paper and glue together at borders. Decorate with teddy bear stickers and outline the cup with thin lace. See template, page 181. Hang a real tea bag out of the cup, and staple a personalized tag to its tag with the birthday child's name (Tea By Angelica).

**Bring a Date**—Invite guests to bring their favorite teddy bears dressed in their finest, too!

## What to Wear

Guests come "dressed for tea" in their prettiest party clothes. Suggest that they wear festive special occasion dresses. Keep this party indoors so guests stay clean!

**A cute touch**—When the guests arrive, paint small, black teddy bear noses on them using non-staining face paint.

## Decoration Ideas

The setting of this party requires a soft, Victorian feel and the decor does not have to be expensive. Scout yard sales, flea markets, and second hand stores for decorations and party favors. Here are things to look for:

| | |
|---|---|
| lace tablecloth | cloth napkins |
| lace items | china tea set |
| doily placemats | long white gloves |
| dainty purses | pretty handkerchiefs |
| old fashioned hats | old trunk (cover with lace shawl) |
| teddy bears | pearl necklaces |

## Games & Activities To Play and Do

**Little Miss Manners**—Teach good manners while eating, such as placing napkins on laps, keeping little mouths closed while chewing, and sitting nicely on chairs. But don't make this activity too serious! Add a bit of silliness to keep the party mood, like showing them how to extend their little pinkie fingers while sipping tea.

**Dress-ups**—Provide clothes and accessories such as evening gowns and dresses, white gloves, long pearls, evening bags, hats, jewelry, and lace collars. Visit yard sales and scan closets to collect used clothing. After the party, give the dress-up box to a charity or preschool, or give it to the birthday girl as a gift.

**Old Fashioned Games**—Kids never tire of the classics. Play a few games such as Gossip, Mother May I, Duck Duck Goose, Simon Says, and Musical Chairs.

**Teddy Bear Fun**—Read a teddy bear story, then play "Pass the Teddy Bear" while playing music. The little girl who is holding the bear when the music stops sits in the middle. Begin the music again. Another person is caught holding the bear when the music stops and replaces the child sitting in the middle.

**Follow the Bear**—Turn three tea cups upside down and place a miniature teddy bear underneath one cup. Move the cups around and let the girls take turns guessing the location of the bear.

## Craft Options

**Happy Masks**—Make teddy bear masks out of paper bags. Provide ribbons, buttons, bows and lace to accessorize.

**Twin Necklaces**—Provide chunky beads and colored cord for the girls to make matching bead necklaces for themselves and their bears. Or, make edible necklaces on pieces of shoestring licorice by stringing Lifesavers, Cheerios, Fruit Loops, pretzel wheels, and any other food with holes.

**Fun Mugs**—Decorate white plastic mugs with markers, decals, stickers, and confetti. Or, buy craft mugs which have removable paper inserts. The kids remove the inserts, color them, and place them back in the mugs.

## Food & Treat Selections

Kids will feel all grown up munching these goodies and sipping tea with their friends and teddys:

| | |
|---|---|
| petit fours | teddy bear shaped cookies |
| flavored iced tea | sugar cubes for the iced tea |
| muffins | finger sandwiches |
| honeydip donuts | biscuits and jelly |
| lemonade | hot chocolate |

## Cake Possibility

Make a teddy bear cake using one round cake pan for the belly, one small round cake pan for the head, Twinkies or Devil Dogs for the arms and legs, and two cupcakes for the ears. Or, make only the head with a round cake pan and cupcake ears.

## Favors To Go

It has been a "tea-rrific" party! Send them home with pretty ceramic tea cups on a saucer. Place teddy bear stickers and teddy bear pins inside. Wrap in netting, and tie with a piece of lace. Other favor ideas include toy tea sets, Victorian paper dolls, teddy bear coloring books, lace handkerchiefs, and Beanie Baby teddy bears.

# The North Pole Expedition

*Short of traveling to the North Pole for winter white fun,*
*you can create a snowy, white setting at your house*
*for a chilly party experience!*

GLUE ON A SEQUIN
SNOWFLAKE FOR A
LITTLE SPARKLE!

NORTH
POLE

ROLL UP
FLIER &
WRAP WITH
A THIN RED
RIBBON

NORTH POLE
PARTY

PLEASE WEAR
MY FAVORITE
COLOR: WHITE!

FOR: _____
DATE: _____
TIME: _____
PLACE: _____

DIRECTIONS:
_____
_____
_____
_____

## The Invitation

**Striped Pole**—Is there really a North Pole? Guests find out when they read this party invitation made on a "North Pole" sign cut out of square pieces of red construction paper. Attach a white rolled-up invitation to the sign to simulate its pole. Wrap the "pole" in thin red ribbon to make candy cane stripes. Give instructions to open the pole to read the party details. See template, page 182.

**Paper Snowflakes**—Write party information on paper snowflakes made out of white construction paper. Add white glitter.

**Party Pets**—Attach rolled party invitations around the necks of stuffed penguins or white bears.

## What to Wear

The guests will be hard to see as they blend in with the white decor of this party. Ask guests to wear all white clothing including hats, belts, shoes and other accessories.

## Decoration Ideas

Create the illusion of a cold, snowy place—the North Pole! What do you see? Lots of white and lots of snow! One or more of the following suggestions can help:

**Snowy Scenery**—Hang handmade snowflakes or paper doilies from the ceiling. Perhaps making paper snowflakes can be an opening activity for guests as they wait for everyone to arrive. Hang posters of skiing and snow scenes around the party area.

**Icy Ice Cubes**—Make fun ice cubes with festive ice cube trays found in party stores.

**Everything's White!**—Use all white party goods: plates, tablecloth, cups, napkins, utensils and balloons.

**Ice Sculpture**—Order an ice sculpture shaped like a mountain, a polar bear, or a penguin.

## Games & Activities To Play and Do

**Marshmallow Balancing**—Take turns balancing marshmallows on each other's foreheads, and back of hands. Try knees and elbows, too!

**Marshmallow Construction**—Build imaginative things out of marshmallows. Provide lots of marshmallows and toothpicks and see what the kids invent!

**Shaving Cream Finger Painting**—Have the kids draw images with their fingers, using shaving cream on dark colored construction paper. The shaving cream hardens as it dries.

**Let It Snow**—Let the kids play outside in the snow, either at the beginning or at the end of the party. While outside, make snow angels and snowmen. Provide scarves, buttons, carrots, corncob pipes, and plastic black hats.

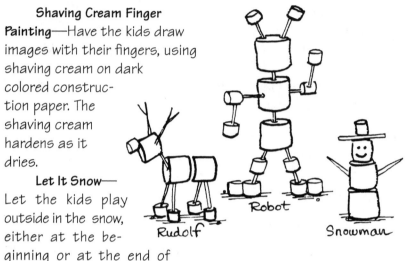

Rudolf

Robot

Snowman

**Penguin Freeze**—To music, kids must waddle like penguins. Everyone has to freeze into position when the music stops. No one can move until the music starts again. This is a just for fun game—don't make anyone "sit out."

**Freeze Tag**—One person is "it." All the kids run away while "it" tries to tag them. When someone is tagged, he has to freeze into position until everyone else is tagged. The game starts over with a new "it."

**Pin the What?**—Make one of these out of poster board or felt: Pin the Bow Tie on the Penguin, Pin the Nose on the Polar Bear, or Pin the Carrot on the Snowman.

**Winter Clothes Relay**—Have two piles of winter clothes and two teams. The first person on each team runs to one pile of clothes and dresses in all of them as quickly as possible. He then takes off the clothes, leaves them in a pile and runs to the back of the line. The second person in line begins dressing, etc. Each team member has to dress and undress, and the first team finished wins. Provide winter clothes such as scarves, adult boots, ski pants, coats, mittens, hats, and sweaters.

**Toilet Paper Relay**—Played in teams, the line leader holds a pencil placed through a roll of white toilet paper (the pencil allows it to roll easily) while the first team member takes the end of the toilet paper and runs through an obstacle course. The object is not to break the ream of paper. Set up a simple obstacle course: walking over a chair, crawling under the kitchen table, circling twice around a column, crawling across the sofa, and going back to the starting line.

# Craft Options

**Styrofoam Snowman**—Hot glue together three different sized styrofoam balls. The bottom ball must be sliced flat on its base so the snowman will stand up. Black tacks can be used for the eyes, mouth and buttons. Provide small pieces of fabric for the scarves. Licorice pipes can be found in candy stores for the snowman's pipe. For the nose, use slices of carrot.

**Snow Globes**—Using baby food jars with lids, glue a miniature snowman figurine inside of each lid. Fill the jars with water and glitter and replace the lids.

**Cool Mittens**—Decorate plain mittens with sequins, gems, felt shapes, or puffy paint.

# Food & Treat Selections

**Think "Cool!"**— Treats for this wintry party can include popsicles, vanilla ice cream, snowballs, whipped topping, vanilla milkshakes (attach mini "North Pole" signs on red/white striped straw), soda floats with vanilla ice cream and clear soda. Then "warm" up everyone with hot chocolate and floating marshmallows.

**Cold Food**—garden salad, shrimp or tuna salad, pickles and olives.

**Snowman Goody**—Freeze these individual treats in advance of the party. In foil cupcake liners, stack one large vanilla ice cream scoop, one medium scoop, and one miniature scoop to create a snowman. Use pretzel sticks for arms, chocolate chips for eyes and mouth, candy corn for nose, and small candies for buttons. Black licorice bites can be used as a hat, or you can find black licorice hat shapes. Cut pieces of Fruit Roll-ups for the scarf.

## Cake Options

**Snowman Cake**—Make a snowman-shaped cake out of three different size round cake pans. Decorate with white icing and coconut. Use chocolate cookies for the eyes and buttons, raisins or chocolate chips for the mouth, and an orange peel for the nose. Add a fabric scarf and black poster board hat.

**Igloo Cake**—Bake a white cake in a round oven-proof bowl. Turn it upside down and cut out an igloo "door." Cover the cake with white icing or whipped topping.

## Favors To Go

Warm up the guests after this chilly party! Fill pairs of mittens or cute mugs with packs of instant hot cocoa. Or, place miniature stuffed penguins or polar bears inside of mittens.

# The Un-Pajama Party

*This evening, bedtime-related party is an almost slumber party. Guests come prepared to spend the night, but they don't! When parents pick up their kids—guess what? All ready for bed!*

The
UN-PAJAMA
PARTY

VICTORIA

FOR
LINDSEY's
7th BIRTHDAY
Saturday, Jan. 8
7 pm - 9 pm.

Please bring an overnite bag with p.j's, robe, slippers, sleeping bag, pillow & your favorite stuffed animal & of course, this toothbrush!

← Fold arm up & glue to brush

Glue →

## The Invitation

**Personal Touch**—Send a personalized toothbrush with each invitation. The outline of the invitation can be a cutout of a nightgown. See template, page 183.

**Hold It**—Send party flyers rolled up in plastic toothbrush holders.

## What to Wear

Invite kids dressed in their pajamas, robes, and slippers. Ask them to bring pillows and sleeping bags, toothbrushes and stuffed animals.

## Decoration Ideas

Make your guests comfy cozy! Cover the entire party area with blankets, pillows, comforters, air mattresses and futons. Also, make blanket forts by draping blankets over chairs and tables. Pop-up tents and play huts can be added for more rolling around, soft fun.

## Games & Activities To Play and Do

Keep the kids busy and tucker them out so they will fall asleep on the way home!

**Slipper Parade**—Have a parade of slippers! Each friend models a pair for the "judges." Select the scariest, cutest, prettiest, and funniest pair. Let each guest win a category.

**Talented Tootsies**—Have a contest to see who can draw the best picture on paper with their toes.

**Memory Mix**—Place ten small objects on a tray like a marble, comb, dice, toy, battery, eraser, candle, pencil, rubber band, and paper clip. Divide the kids into two or three teams. Let kids study the objects for a minute, then cover them. See how many items the kids can recall by having each team make a list. If the children are too young to write, have them call out the items.

**Hoppy Relay**—Have relay races by hopping in pillow cases. Be sure to clear a large area so no one will get hurt.

**Movie Moment**—Play a popular movie on the VCR or order a Pay-Per-View movie.

**Story Time**—Tell a bedtime story or listen to a story on tape (this depends on the age group).

**Teeth-Brushing Jam**—Before leaving, the group must brush their teeth. Provide bubble gum toothpaste, colorful bathroom cups and paper hand towels. See who can brush the longest. See who can sing a song while they brush.

# Craft Options

**Bookmarks**—Provide precut bookmarks of light colored card stock. Let kids decorate with stickers, markers and rubber stamps. Attach small tassels on the side of each bookmark and cover with clear contact paper.

**Autographed Memento**—Decorate a white pillowcase and have each guest sign it for the birthday child.

# Food & Treat Selections

**Breakfast Bites**—They won't have room in their tummies for breakfast the next morning after this menu. Serve breakfast foods such as donuts, toaster pastries, eggs, bacon, sausage, toast, and cereal.

**Self-Servers**—Kids like to do it themselves. Set up one or all of the following:

**Milk and Cookies Buffet:**
- strawberry and chocolate milk mix
- an assortment of cookies with dips: chocolate, icing, sprinkles
- fun and colorful cups, straws, plates and napkins

**Ice Cream Sundae Bar**—See page 15 for ingredients.

**Juice Bar**—A juice bar can offer a variety of flavored juices like orange, pineapple, apple, V-8, cranberry and grapefruit juices. Fruit drinks can also be included. For fun, provide maraschino cherries, colorful straws and cups, paper umbrellas, and lemons and limes.

## Cake Possibilities

**Toothbrush Cake**—Cut a cake in the shape of a toothbrush out of a rectangular cake pan. For the bristles, select one of these options: small pieces of shoestring licorice, thin peppermint sticks, or candles.

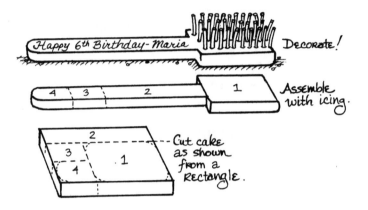

Happy 6th Birthday - Maria    Decorate!

4  3  2  1    Assemble with icing.

2
3  1
4    Cut cake as shown from a Rectangle.

**P.J. Cake**—Decorate a rectangular cake with an illustration of a pair of pajamas if you are artistic or ask a bakery to design it.

## Favors To Go

The guests are ready to be tucked in! Send them home with these items tucked in kiddie cereal bowls: bubblegum toothpaste, personalized toothbrushes, cute kiddie cups, story books, miniature cereal boxes, and kiddie spoons.

# The Cookie Caper

For a nice, cozy indoors party on a cold day,
fill your house with the scrumptious baking aroma of
cookies! This party will involve the guests as you
distribute jobs of making, baking and eating one of
America's favorite—the cookie!

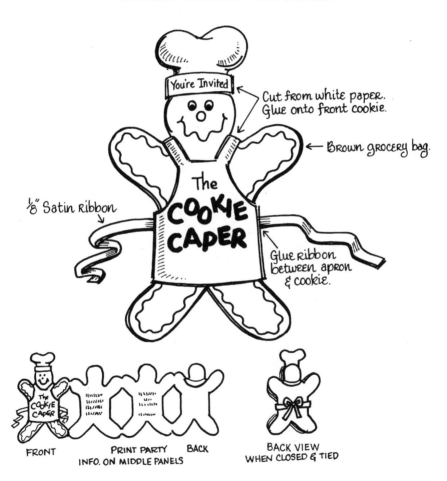

You're Invited

Cut from white paper.
Glue onto front cookie.

← Brown grocery bag.

⅛" Satin ribbon

The COOKIE CAPER

Glue ribbon
between apron
& cookie.

FRONT

PRINT PARTY INFO. ON MIDDLE PANELS

BACK

BACK VIEW
WHEN CLOSED & TIED

## The Invitation

**Gingerbread String**—Make gingerbread men out of brown grocery bags. Cut out the shape from four layers of brown paper, so that when you open up the invitation, it becomes a string of gingerbread men. Add white baker's hats and aprons on the leading gingerbread man. Add pieces of ribbon as the apron strings and tie them in the back of the invitations. Party details will be written inside. See template, page 184.

**What's the Recipe?**—Send the invitation written as a cookie recipe, such as:

### A "Cookie Caper" Recipe

*Ingredients*
10  *eight year old kids*
 1  *dozen eggs*
    *lots of sugar and flour*
 3  *cups chef's hats*
 5  *tsp. aprons*
    *cookie sheets*

Directions: Combine kids, aprons and hats on May 15th. Add eggs, sugar and flour. Place on cookie sheets at 5 Sparks Avenue. Bake from 2:00 to 4:00 p.m. in Elle's [birthday child's name] oven for a delicious birthday party. Cool slightly before sending home. Yields 10 happy kids.

**What To Bring**—Ask guests to bring their favorite cookie recipes (enough copies for each guest) to make the cookbook craft as described on page 92. Also, invite guests to bring two dozen cookies to the party for a cookie exchange (see Activities).

## What to Wear

To get everyone into the spirit of baking cookies and to protect their clothing while in the kitchen, invite guests to wear aprons to the party. Provide hair nets or paper baker's hats.

## Decoration Ideas

**Bright Bakery**—A festive kitchen it shall be! Decorate the baking equipment with ribbons and colorful shredded paper until you are ready to use them: mixing bowls, mixer, spatulas, cookie sheets, measuring cups, and other baking utensils.

**Cheerful Chart**—Make a chart on a large piece of poster board, indicating jobs for each guest, such as loading the dishwasher, wiping the counter, setting the table, and licking the beaters!

**Placemats**—Make to look like gingerbread cookies by using brown construction paper or brown grocery bags and white chalk or crayon.

## Games & Activities To Play and Do

**Busy Baking**—Let the kids assemble the cookie wreath as described on page 104. Or, preassemble ingredients to bake one or two types of cookies, and assist the guests with the recipe and the decorating (provide sprinkles and writing gel). Let an adult place the cookie sheets into the oven.

**Cookie Exchange**—Guests swap the cookies which they brought to the party. Everyone takes home the same number of cookies that they brought.

**Sniff and Name**—Blindfold each participant and have her name the ingredient or food being placed under her nose. Use items such as chocolate, icing, vanilla, milk, butter, flour, and a cookie.

**The Gingerbread Man**—Bake gingerbread cookies in advance, then provide white icing in decorating tubes so the kids can add the trimming.

**The Big Cookie**—Make one large cookie in advance for each guest. Kids can decorate using sprinkles, m&m's, and colored icing and gel in decorating tubes.

## Craft Options

**Pretty Aprons**—Decorate white aprons with fabric paint, permanent markers or by sponge painting.

**Very Own Cookbook**—Provide materials such as construction paper, yarn, markers, and a hole punch to make personalized cookbook covers. The contents of the cookbook will be made up of one of each recipe brought by party guests.

**Hat Decorating**—Garnish paper baker's hats with markers, stickers and rubber stamps.

**Crazy Cookies**—Let kids create their own cookie and its recipe. Divide them into groups and have them "name" their cookie creation and write down its ingredients. Encourage silly!

## Food & Treat Selections

They can't eat only cookies in this kitchen! Fill up the hungry bakers with some of these:

**Make Your Own Pizza**—Using large cookie cutters, cut out pieces of pizza dough (or refrigerator biscuits) and let kids make personalized pizzas with sauce, cheese and toppings.

**Sandwich Cuts**—Cookie cutters can also be used to cut bread for peanut butter and jelly, egg salad and tuna fish sandwiches.

**Cookie Pizza**—Bake a giant cookie using a package of cookie dough. When cool, spread with whipped topping and add kiwi and strawberries. Dribble chocolate on top.

**Milk and Cookies Buffet**—see page 87.

## Cake Possibility

**Cookie Wreath**—On a large baking sheet, drop teaspoons of cookie dough in the shape of a wreath. Decorate with sprinkles or other toppings and follow baking directions for the cookie recipe. Add a ribbon to the top of the wreath when it cools.

## Favors To Go

Time to get cookin'! Send off the little bakers with clear measuring cups with small baking accessories inside, like decorative sprinkles and cookie cutters. Wrap in colored plastic wrap and use colored raffia to attach measuring spoons.

Other favor ideas include toy baking accessories, holiday cookie recipe books, gift certificates for "The Great Cookie," small tins of cookies, or kiddie cookies such as animal crackers or bear-shaped treats.

# Giggles 'n Grins

**This funny, giddy and giggly party will have guests chuckling and snickering long after party's end. Silly is encouraged!**

## The Invitation

Smile!—This party theme will bring a smile to friends' faces as they receive their invitation. Write party details on a round smile face made out of yellow poster board and black marker. Insert a large tongue (made from construction paper) through a slit in the smile and write the party details on it. See template, page 185. On the back of the invitation, write a silly joke or riddle. Invite guests to bring their favorite jokes to the party.

HA-HA!—Draw the words "HA-HA" in block letters on colored card stock, and cut out. Party details are written directly on the words. See template, page 186.

## What to Wear

Start everyone laughing the moment they arrive! Invite guests to dress in bizarre color combinations and mismatched patterns— almost clown-like. For instance, striped shirts and checked pants would do the trick; so would colorful hats, socks and suspenders.

## Decoration Ideas

**Smiles On You**—Everywhere guests look, they'll find a smile! Hang, place, and scatter yellow smile faces all around the party room.

**Laughing People**—Make collages of laughing people out of magazine pictures. Adhere to poster board. This activity can be handled by the birthday child before the party.

**Funny Placemats**—Make from newspaper "funnies" glued or taped to rectangular pieces of cardboard. Cover tightly with clear plastic wrap or clear contact paper. These also can be laminated at an office supply store or a copy center.

**Entertainment**—Hire a silly children's party entertainer such as a clown or a comical magician.

## Games & Activities To Play and Do

**Funny Face**—Take instant pictures of the kids making funny faces as they arrive. Display the photos on a large piece of poster board attached to the refrigerator with magnets. Give the pictures to the kids as take home favors.

**Joke Contest**—Since each guest brought his/her favorite joke, have a joke telling contest and give prizes for the best joke, funniest joke, grossest joke, dumbest joke, etc. Make sure everyone wins a category.

**Make Us Laugh**—While seated in a circle on the floor, take turns making funny faces and let the kids vote for the best one. Ask parents to join in too!

**Stone Face**—One person must keep a straight face while another tries to make him/her laugh. Variation: stare at each other for one minute without cracking a smile.

**What's So Funny?**—While timing them, have kids make lists of things in life that make them laugh and smile. See who can list the most. The sillier the better!

# Craft Options

**Create-A-Face**—Provide white or light colored T-shirts with oval faces already drawn on them. Provide fabric markers to decorate the faces. Kids take home the shirts.

**Putty Transfers**—Provide Silly Putty and the comics section of the newspaper. Kids will enjoy transferring the comics onto the putty as they press it against the newspaper.

# Food & Treat Selections

At this table, kids <u>are</u> allowed to play with their food!

**Funny Food**—Provide bowls of the following food and let kids make funny faces: bread, raisins, licorice, pretzels, veggies, orange slices, and cherries.

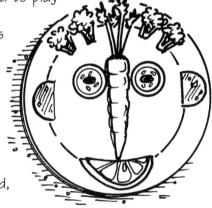

**Silly Faces**—Serve hot dogs and burgers decorated with funny faces using mustard, ketchup, relish, and pickles.

## Cake Possibility

Here's an easy yet fun cake to make. For a smile face cake, decorate a round cake with yellow icing. Use two chocolate cookies for the eyes. Make a smile out of a piece of black shoestring licorice.

## Favors To Go

Send them home laughing! They won't be able to keep a straight face with these goodies: Silly Putty, smile face trinkets (key chain, stickers, change purse), sticker books that create funny faces, toys that shake and giggle, joke books, plastic nose/eyeglasses ensembles. Check out gag gift stores for more laughable items.

# Rough Sketch Ideas . . . More Kids' Themes

**Now it's your turn to be creative and clever! Here are a few rough ideas to get you started in creating a theme party.**

## Airport Party

Up, up and away! Let's fly through this party! Inquire at a local airport about a party room for little pilots. Maybe the kids can tour behind the scenes. Send either a passport or a paper airplane invitation. Ask one of the airlines for plastic wing pins, airline peanuts, napkins and/or any other favor with their logo. Fill a small travel bag with favors such as toy airplanes, parachute men, and gliders.

## Back to School Party

It's back to school so soon! These students wish summer wasn't over, so cheer them up by hosting a party on the first day of school. Invite kids to get off the bus with your child. Set out a large bowl of red apples. Play a drawing guessing game using school related clues like lunchbox, chalkboard, pencil, teacher. Prizes for games can be fun school supplies (funky pens, pencil tops or decorative folders). Draw a school bus on the cake, outlined with black shoestring licorice. Make sure to sing, "The People on the Bus Go Up and Down!" Give favors in a cute pencil pouch or colored lunchbag.

## Biking Party

Pedal pushers, get ready for a healthy ride! Meet party guests with their bikes at a local biking trail. Helmets required! Before the ride, let the kids decorate their bikes and helmets with streamers, crepe paper, balloons and cards clipped with clothes pins to the spokes (remember that?) to give the bike "sound." Pack a big picnic lunch, and stop after a few miles to have the birthday party on a grassy area. Play easy outside games (which require no equipment) such as Simon Says, Mother May I, and Hide 'n Seek. Then ride back to the starting place. Favors can be cute squeaky bike horns in animal shapes, small bike bags, or biking gloves. You can also plan this idea at your house and parade through the neighborhood on the decorated bikes.

## Craft Party

These crafty critters will have fun creating something new at this party! Check with a local craft, fabric or hardware store for available kids' classes in ceramics, decoupage, painting, sewing, basket weaving, jewelry making, mask making, plaster craft, birdhouse making, doll making, etc. The store will usually set up a private room for the party so you can bring gifts and a cake.

## Cowboy Bob Party

Yeeha!! Ride 'em cowboy! Young cowpokes will be adorned in paper bag vests with fringed ends—decorate with markers and crayons and add a sheriff's badge. Make rattlesnakes out of rope: use cardboard for the head; use a film container filled with rice for the rattler's tail. Blindfolded, "hunt in the hay" for small toy prizes. Have lasso practice with a hula hoop and a toy horse. Use squirt guns to move balloons along in a relay race. Line snack bowls with bandanas. Favors can include cowboy hats, bandanas, harmonicas, and trail mix.

## Double Digit Party

It's a double take! This party is for a double digit age, like 10, 11, 12, etc. Plan everything in doubles: mail two invitations, serve two cakes, sing happy birthday twice, serve two drinks and two hot dogs, play games twice, say everything two times, pair up kids, etc.

## Down on the Farm Party

Old McDonald had a farm, E-I-E-I-O. And on this farm he had a party! Offer pony rides, hayrides, and a petting zoo. Provide straw hats and ask the little farmers to wear overalls and work-boots. Provide supplies to make scarecrows. Make "pigs in a blanket"—hot dogs cut in half and wrapped and baked in refrigerator dough. Play the game, "Noah's Search" as described on page 41.

## Earth Angel Party

Angels fly because they take themselves lightly! Little angels attend this party dressed in angel costumes, or wearing white. Serve angel food cake and angel shaped cookies. Make angel wings out of coat hangers covered with pantyhose, white spray paint and glitter. Make a favor bag to simulate an angel: white lunch bag folded at top, fold paper doily over top to simulate wings; add round paper face; use curly ribbon for hair.

## First Decade Party

There's a first time for everything! This party is for the kid who is turning age 10. Plan everything in 10's: 10 guests, 10 games (earn 10 points while doing 10 jumps, 10 laps, 10 balls in a basket), 10 small cakes, sing Happy Birthday 10 times, 10 gifts, 10 favors, etc. Decorate with 10's! Have the party at 10:00 on the 10th of the month.

## Indy 500 Party

Varooommmmm . . . start your engines! With black poster board and white paint or crayon, set up a "road" at this party entrance for arriving race car drivers. Use orange cones and flags. Set up a toy racetrack. Hang posters of Indy 500 and Daytona, and pictures of race car drivers. Make race cars from cardboard boxes. Favors can include automobile related stickers, race cars, toy cars, and car racing magazines.

## Mystical Mermaid Party

If I lived under the sea! The color scheme for this mermaid party is aqua blue and seafoam green. Make-believe mermaids can wear swimsuits. Decorate the party area with mermaids, fish, octopus, sea creatures, and sand dollars. Provide seashells to decorate with glitter and gems. Watch a movie about a mermaid or a dolphin. Have a scavenger hunt for things you find under the sea: crabs, lobsters, and treasure (use chocolate gold coins and plastic crustaceans). Use mesh bags to collect scavenger hunt items.

## A Sailor Went to Sea-Sea-Sea Party

Ahoy Matey! These little sailors wear all white or nautical attire. Provide sailor hats. Hire a Popeye mascot. Decorate with a nautical decor. Play "Pin the Spinach Can on Popeye." Make sailboats from styrofoam meat trays and straws (see page 75). Make newspaper sailor hats. Put a fake tattoo on each kid. Set up an inflatable boat with oars. Serve boat sandwiches from hollowed out dinner rolls; add a paper sail on a toothpick.

# Kids' Party Alternatives

In lieu of having a kids' birthday party at a run-of-the-mill party location, consider an educational location. Think "field trip." Check the yellow pages to see what local factories, plants, community buildings, and manufacturers in your area are open for tours.

Educational party locations:

| | | |
|---|---|---|
| candy factory | graphics company | greenhouse |
| pet store | automobile factory | historical site |
| book printing plant | hospital | museum |
| soap factory | post office | nature center |
| bakery | pumpkin farm | dentist's office |
| toy factory | grocery store | police station |

Alternative locations to host a party:

| | | |
|---|---|---|
| gymnastics studio | park and playground | circus |
| carnival | nature trail | children's theater |
| bike trail | sporting event | karate studio |
| berry picking farm | farm | campground |
| skating rink | pool or quarry | bowling alley |
| fast food restaurant | zoo | wall climbing facility |
| airport | hardware store | craft or fabric store |

Alternative items to use instead of favor bags:

| | | |
|---|---|---|
| beach buckets | water bottles | birthday hats |
| mittens | planters | peat pots |
| cosmetic bags | colorful containers | lunchboxes |
| hats | tea cups | measuring cups |
| kitchen aprons | carpenter aprons | popcorn bags |
| fish bowls | masks | cereal bowls |

Shop in a dollar store for alternative containers to fit your theme.

# Tips for Kids' Parties

## *If you are the Hostess . . .*

**Who Else is Invited?**—Let parents know who is invited to your child's party so they have the opportunity to car pool. Also indicate on children's invitations whether parents should drop off or stay with their child.

**Not Too Many**—Keep the number of guests simple and most likely your party will run smoothly without overwhelming your child. Inviting every child in the class, scout troop and neighborhood is only inviting a few hours of chaotic frenzy for you. This is especially true if you are hosting a sleepover.

**Not Inside**—Consider your garage or unfinished basement to hold a kids' party. The concrete floor is a great place to begin decorating—draw pictures according to your theme using colored chalk (mops up easily).

**Bulk Supplies**—To save money, visit a wholesale store to purchase candy, snacks, favors, soda and paper goods in bulk.

**Homemade Tablecloth**—Cover the party table with white butcher paper and let the party guests color and decorate it with stickers, rubber stamps, markers and crayons to match the party theme. This is a good opening activity.

**Little Bodies, Little Chairs**—Use child-sized tables and chairs for kids' parties. Borrow from friends or neighbors if you don't have enough for all the guests.

**Ouch!**—Have a first aid kit handy, just in case of boo-boos!

**Special Plate**—Purchase a "special birthday plate" for your family. Each time someone has a birthday, receives an award, wins a championship, or celebrates a special event, s/he has the privilege of using the special plate for meals and a piece of celebration cake.

**Ask and You Shall Receive!**—Don't be shy to ask vendors and establishments for free items that may fit your theme, such as popcorn bags, samples, promotional items, displays, etc. You may be surprised at their generosity.

**Label Everything**—Write names on cups, favor bags, crafts and prizes, labeling ahead of time when you can. Hand out favors as the children leave.

**Thanks in Advance**—Attach a note from the birthday child on each party favor bag, thanking each child for the gift and for attending.

**Homemade Stickers**—Decorate favor bags and invitation envelopes by cutting out designs from decorative contact paper.

**Craft Sample**—Make a sample craft ahead of time to show children. Save time by purchasing precut craft materials.

**Opening Activity**—Kids are less apt to run wild if you provide an immediate activity at the beginning of the party.

**"I Don't Want To"**—It's okay if a child does not want to participate in a specific activity, craft or game. Some children feel more comfortable as observers.

**Everyone Wins**—"Winning" and "losing" games are not recommended because they can invite tears. Let everyone participate in every game. Try not to play games that make kids sit out.

**Will They Be Fed?**—If you will be feeding children pizza, hot dogs or something substantial other than cake and ice cream, indicate this on the invitation.

**Number Cake**—Make a cake in the shape of your child's age. From a rectangular cake, cut out the appropriate numeral(s). Hold together with icing and decorate with festive sprinkles and cake accessories. Instead of birthday candles, use sparklers!

### *If you are the guest . . .*

**Sorry, No Siblings**—Leave other children at home if you are planning to stay at a birthday party with your child. The hostess may not have enough "extras" and your little one may feel left out of the festivities.

**Drop-off or Stay?**—Assume that you are to drop off your child to a party, unless s/he is very young. Hosting parents may not be expecting extra adults to hang around.

**Pick-Up on Time**—Be on time when picking up your child from a birthday party. By party's end, the hosting parents are usually ready to wrap it up.

**Don't Ask**—Tell your child not to ask for an extra favor bag to take home for a sibling. The hostess may not be prepared with enough.

# Teen Time

Theme party ideas
for teenagers ages 12 to 17

# Teenager of Mine

*Teenager of mine,*
*Oh how you shine!*
*Since your first cry,*
*How quickly, quickly it all went by!*

*Your first date,*
*"Okay, but not great."*
*"Oh, really?" I state,*
*(Thank goodness . . . way too young to mate!)*

*Your grades are super!*
*Your smile is a winner.*
*Everyday you get prettier,*
*More grown up and thinner.*

*A concert? A movie with friends?*
*Out you go until 11 p.m.*
*I can see this is just the beginning,*
*Not even close to the end.*

*Driving? Are you serious?*
*That thought makes me delirious!*
*You take your test and pass,*
*Yet you can't afford your own gas.*

*Your ring ceremony is here,*
*Then the senior prom until dawn.*
*And next this boyfriend of yours*
*Passes out on the front lawn.*

*Now it's time to make a college choice.*
*I can hardly see, my eyes are moist.*
*Graduation - what a big day!*
*Another step along life's way.*

*"Oh Mother! I will need all this gear*
*To outfit my dorm!"*
*What happened to this last year?*
*Were we swept up in a storm?*

*Seventeen, 18, 19, 20,*
*Leaving home without any money.*
*Now I see it is all your choice.*
*I guess you really do have your own voice.*

*All teenager, all grown up.*
*Tell me, where did the time fly?*
*Who knew during it all,*
*It would so quickly pass . . . sigh . . . Goodbye.*

by book author
Bernadette A. Moyer
Two-Bee-A-Twin-Bee Publishing
Lutherville, Maryland

*A*dolescence is a funny era for parents to deal with in kids' lives. Young teens want to fit in, be cool, and impress their friends. When it comes to celebrating their birthdays, some teens may feel that they are too grown up to have a birthday party at home. They may prefer to have a birthday celebration "off site" at a "cool" location. Others may prefer not to be in the spotlight at all and may want their birthday to pass unnoticed. And some may not care what you plan, as long as you definitely make it a big deal and celebrate in a way that interests them.

For whatever type of teenager you are planning for, you're sure to find a clever idea in this section to suit their tastes and whims. Written in mind for the teenager between the ages of 12 and 17, these 25 party ideas and 30 fun places to host a party may assist you in deciding how to celebrate another year of adolescence!

# Teen Time

## All Night Horror Show

Teens will remember this 'horror'ible party experience! Everyone brings his or her favorite horror movie and dresses up as its main character. Have a video jam by watching the horror movies all night long! Decorate with monster decor and make slime punch: mix powdered green drink mix and float green gelatin cubes in it. Add green ice cubes which can be made with food coloring or add gummy worms. Freeze edible eyeballs or bugs in the ice cubes.

## Backward Progressive Combo

Teens can get bored easily. Don't add to their boredom with a humdrum party. Spice up a birthday with this Backward Progressive Combination party. This is no ordinary birthday party! Combine your teen's party with a few of her friends who share birthdays in the same month. Everyone must dress with all of their clothes on backwards. Begin at one teen's house with dessert, in this case, birthday cake. Open the gifts first, then sing happy birthday, then make a wish, then light the candle. Continue the celebration at another teen's house for an appetizer and refreshments. Then, on to a third teen's house for the main meal. Add more "stops" for games, a movie, whatever! No structure is needed for this chaotic party that doesn't stand still!

## Big Screen

Your teen is the star of this show! Take a group to the movies dressed as movie stars. A "cool" touch would be to rent a limo! The invitation could resemble a movie ticket. Have the cake made to look like a big screen with your teen's name "in lights" and silhouettes of movie seats in the foreground. Ask the theater if they have a party room. Provide each guest with a bag of popcorn, box of candy, and a soda for the movie.

## Bus Trippin'

Teenagers won't want to miss this bus! Pick an interesting bus destination that appeals to teens like an amusement park, snow skiing, or a trip to New York City. Surprise the guest of honor with a bunch of friends as s/he gets on the bus, and then celebrate with a bus party. Decorate the bus, play games, tell jokes on the speaker, serve snacks, etc.

## Chocolate Fest

Satisfy that sweet tooth! For the chocolate lover's birthday, what better theme than a Chocolate Fest! Invite guests to dress in all brown clothes. Send chocolate kisses with the invitations or glue a piece of paper with the party details on the inside of chocolate wrappers. Serve everything chocolate including chocolate milk, chocolate cake, chocolate licorice, chocolate candy. Make a chocolate dipping station with pretzels, pineapple chunks, and strawberries dipped into melted chocolate.

## Dancin' Fools

Let's dance, boogie and rock 'n roll! Rent a small hall to host a dance for your teen. Hire a deejay, set up karaoke, have a dance contest, teach line dancing, do swing dancing, coordinate group games such as limbo, pass the orange neck to neck, the broom trick (boy/girl stand back to back, both holding a broom stick lengthwise between them. They must maneuver their bodies to face each other while not letting go of the broom). Ask the deejay for other game suggestions which may correlate to specific songs.

## Day Camp

Wanted—happy campers! Go camping for the day at a local campground. Hike on a nature trail, find and decorate walking sticks, have a picnic, make s'mores, play games, make crafts, and lay out in the sun. Stay until the evening and sing around the campfire.

## Drag Queens

Just for fun, wouldn't a group of young guys have a blast with this idea? Invite them to a Drag Queen party all dressed in drag! They will get a kick out of trying to apply lipstick, put on panty-hose, and walking in high heels. You could make this a surprise party for your teen who would certainly get the surprise of his life walking into a room where all of his friends are transformed!

## Field Day

It's a field day! Host this party at a local park with a pavilion and an open field. Play softball and frisbee, coordinate team races, and cook burgers and hot dogs on the grill. Have guests bring blankets to spread on the ground and whatever games and gadgets they want to play.

## Food Feast

Mmmmm, mmmmm, good! Depending on what food is popular in your region, host a feast centered around it, like a crab feast, a lobster feast, a clam bake, or a Texas barbecue. For instance, at a crab feast, serve

steamed crabs, corn on the cob, and crab soup, and maybe even non-alcoholic beer or root beer. This party will work best on an outside deck. Hang fun shaped party lights or use yard torches.

## From the Heart

It is better to give than receive. Instead of a party, a generous teen might like to invite guests to the grocery or wholesale store to purchase items for the needy. As a group, guests decide what to buy and to which charity the goods should be donated. Purchases may include toys for a children's home, books for a literacy center, or personal necessities for a homeless shelter or nursing home. Give them a budget to follow for this project. The guests then wrap the items, and visit the receiving charity to present them.

## Happy Hour

What time is it? It's "Happy Hour!" Plan this party at your house from 4:00 to 6:00 p.m. Make tasty alcohol-free drinks like Bloody Marys, Pina Coladas, White Russians, non-alcoholic beer, etc. Serve happy hour finger foods such as hot buffalo wings and celery, pizza bites, and miniature egg rolls. Set up music and a dance area.

## Haunted Evening

Boo! Witches and goblins won't scare this group. If your teen's birthday is around Halloween, a birthday celebration might include taking a group on a spooky hayride or haunted house sponsored by a local organization. Afterwards, spend the night in a scary place, like the woods!

## Lock-in

No one can leave and no one can sleep! Rent a small community hall for a group campout and an all-night party. Play games, serve pizza, dance, and make crafts. In the morning, go outside to see the sun rise!

## The Mall Quest

What's one favorite destination for a teen? The mall! This idea provides the perfect setting for a teen celebration. Invite a group of friends to participate for your teen's birthday. As a surprise, have everyone meet at the mall to participate in a scavenger hunt. Some malls have community rooms where you may be able to set up the cake and gifts. Be sure to alert the mall management office that you are planning this event. You may want to have identification buttons or hats made up for everyone to wear so the group can be identified easily by mall shoppers and store personnel.

This scavenger hunt must be well organized and arranged ahead of time. Divide the group into teams. Ask each team to decide on a team name. Clues for the scavenger hunt can be handled in two different ways:

1) Provide each team with a list of things to do and find, or
2) Teams must find a series of clues in various stores throughout the mall.

If you choose the first option, each team must have an instant camera and a few dollars. Here is an example of a requirement to include on the list:

> Find a total stranger, any will do
> Get them to wear red lipstick for you.
> This one is easy, is that what you said?
> Oh, by the way, their hair must be red!

The kids will have to first buy red lipstick, find a redhead, then ask this stranger to put on the lipstick and pose for a picture.

List silly things to do, inexpensive products to purchase, pictures to take, things to make, things to figure out. The sillier the better! Know which stores are in the mall so the ideas work well. Here are some examples of silly things to add to the list, or invent your own!

Bring back the following instant pictures:

- someone in your group kissing a frog
- team member doing a handstand in front of a fountain wearing a fake mustache
- all team members in one public bathroom stall at the same time
- female in group with the longest hair balancing a spoon on her nose
- team member tossing pizza dough in the air behind a pizza counter
- male team member dressed in an evening gown or woman's bathing suit
- two team members on a coin-operated kiddie ride

Bring back these items:

- a handmade necklace made from any three materials
- autographs of five people whose names begin with a 'B'
- everyone must return with fake tattoos in a visible place on body
- a full pack of matches with a name of a restaurant
- a pair of chopsticks
- any U.S. currency dated before 1975
- a practical joke (fly in ice, trick candles, etc.)
- a golf tee

Find these answers:

- How many fountain heads are in the middle of the mall?
- What is the name of an item found in the food court containing rice, avocado and seaweed?

- What is the soup of the day at the restaurant at the south end of the mall?
- What is the middle name of the store manager at the department store at the west end of the mall?
- What is the price of the women's suit in the upper level display window next to the card store?

If you plan the hunt according to the second option listed above (finding a series of clues in various stores) then each group will be given a slip of paper with the first clue at the beginning of the hunt. Each team will receive a different clue so they start at different points in the mall. Make the clues rhyme for added silliness.

Make arrangements ahead of time with the mall stores you choose. Ask permission to tape index cards (clues) to store front windows. Here is an example of a clue:

> In the largest store at the mall's end
> Is a store manager, his name is Ken.
> Visit his office, don't forget to say please
> As you ask him to pose and say "cheese!"

Kids will have to find the right store, seek out the manager, pose for a picture (with the instant camera) and bring it back with the other requirements. You will have asked permission from the store manager ahead of time who will also give out the next clue:

> This store has live things of all kinds,
> Visit it to find your rhyme.
> And while you're there, don't forget,
> Bring back something with a picture of a pet.

Kids will have to go to the pet store and ask the clerk for a bag, or purchase something with a picture of a pet. There they will find their next clue. And so on.

Ideas are limitless for stunts and clues. Take a walk around the mall before this event to spark your creativity and gather ideas. Set a few rules:

- Set a time limit for the scavenger hunt.
- Team members must stay with their assigned group.
- No phone calls to stores to find out answers.
- Kids will agree to follow mall rules and policies, respect store property and other shoppers, and behave appropriately.
- The winner is the first team back to the meeting place who has met all of the requirements.

## Midnight Madness

It's bowling mania as you take a group on a bowling binge! Many bowling alleys invite groups to bowl starting at midnight. Some lanes cater to teens by featuring environments such as bowling under black lights or "Cosmic Bowl," and "Rock 'n Bowl."

## On Stage

What a production! Check your local office of promotion and tourism to see what events are coming to your area: concerts, plays, and festivals. Surprise your teen with tickets to a concert they would enjoy, or take them to a street festival.

## Piercing Binge

Another hole? Piercing is popular with teenagers. Take a group of teens to the mall to get second or third holes pierced in their ears or, in the cartilage at the top of the ear, which is a current craze. Make two rules: 1) one ear piercing per person; 2) they must have parents' written permission. You may want to verbally confirm parental permission as well.

## Pretty Party

Pretty as a picture! Take a group of girls to a hair or cosmetic salon for an afternoon of beauty. Let them select one or two of the following services: facial, manicure, pedicure, haircut, hair braiding, or makeover. Ask one of the beauticians to teach the girls a new braid style, or how to apply makeup. Make sure to take a group picture after everyone is beautified!

## Shore Fun

Teens will "shore" have fun at a beach house for a full weekend of celebrating. Host an overnighter at your shore home (or vacation condo in the mountains.) Make yourself scarce in another room while the teens enjoy a bit of independence in the main room. Let the group choose an excursion during the weekend, like shopping, the movies, a ferry ride, or an amusement park.

## Sleepless Pajama Party

No one is allowed to sleep at this party! And beware to those who do! Who knows what the other guests may do . . . paint their toenails black, tie ribbons to their toes, smear shaving cream on their face, or put their hand in warm water! Play "Truth or Dare," tell ghost stories, eat junk food, and watch favorite movies.

## Splashin' Spree

Wet and wild is the theme of this water party held at your home, swim club, water park, or a public swimming hole. Name the party 'Beach Blanket Bash' and decorate with beach stuff: umbrellas, beach balls, rafts, tubes, sand, an inflatable boat. Hire a deejay. Set up volleyball and badminton courts.

## Spoof Party

That's kids' stuff! Make fun of a current toddler or kid craze which may annoy teens such as a popular doll, a stuffed animal or a t.v. show. Make up games related to that craze such as bobbing for doll parts in a tub full of water. Make sure that no one in the group still likes that specific toy to avoid hurting anyone's feelings.

## Sports Folly

Teens love sports, especially guys. Celebrate his birthday at the "big game" (baseball, lacrosse, football, soccer, ice hockey, basketball) held at a local college or professional sports arena. Arrange ahead of time for the stadium to post a happy birthday message on the scoreboard. Provide soda and candy for each guest.

## Toga! Toga!

This party idea is a real ice breaker. Invite everyone to dress in a toga costume. Then rent the movie "Animal House," and if you have a sense of humor, let them have a food fight! Hire a deejay and make sure to dance to the song, "Shout!"

## Tough Tournaments

Let the games begin! Planned around whatever sport interests your teen, set up a tournament for the party guests: billiards, ping-pong, golf, volleyball, softball, video games, or handheld electronic games.

Or, you can set up sports stations throughout the backyard like a soccer shootout, basketball bounce, hole in one, etc. Guests accumulate points to win prizes, such as gift certificates for fast food restaurants, malls, and music stores, or arcade tokens and movie passes.

## Fun Facilities

Still stumped on a place to host your teen's party? Consider one of these in your area:

| | | |
|---|---|---|
| laser tag | Japanese restaurant | athletic club |
| paint ball | roller skating rink | Broadway show |
| batting cages | ethnic restaurant | science center |
| sports center | coffee house | ice skating show |
| video arcade | indoor soccer field | aquarium |
| carnival | ice skating rink | memorabilia cafe |
| rental hall | restaurant party room | comedy club |
| craft store | ski resort | go-kart park |
| miniature golf | golf driving range | drive-in movies |
| water park | indoor rock climbing | campground |

## Autographed Birthday Memento

How clever! Provide a memento related to the party theme for guests to autograph and give to the birthday teen. A few items that can be autographed include:

- bowling party—a bowling pin (ask for one at the bowling alley)
- field day—a softball or frisbee
- PJ party—a white pillowcase (have them decorate it, too)
- ice show, theater or concert—an admission ticket
- pool party— a beach ball

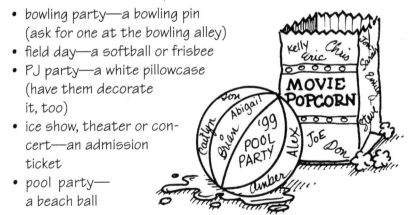

- movie party—a popcorn bag
- sports related party—appropriate ball
- restaurant party—a menu
- coffee house party—a coffee mug
- ski resort party—a lift ticket
- drag queen party—a high heel shoe

For any party: provide a white T-shirt and fabric markers; friends can autograph and decorate the shirt with graffiti while the birthday teen is wearing it. Or, provide a tube of lipstick; everyone puts on the lipstick, kisses the shirt and autographs it.

# Party Cheer Throughout the Year

## Adult party themes
## for every month

# January's
# 'Chill'ebration Winterfest

## A party to lift the spirits and cure cabin fever

Usually, January is a slow social time after the craziness of the holidays. Pep it up by planning a Winterfest! You may decide on a mellow get-together on a Saturday or Sunday afternoon for everyone to simply chill out, or plot a more spirited party for the evening, with or without the kids. If the weather is snowy or icy, organize a neighbors' party so no one has to drive in bad conditions. If you decide on a kid-free zone, arrange for a few babysitters to sit in a neighboring house while the adults enjoy the party at your house.

## Admission to the Winterfest

**Micro-Brew**—An alternative name for this party could be "Micro-Brew Winterfest." Guests bring "admission" of a six-pack of their favorite micro-brew. Place beer in a big tub or kiddie pool with ice, accessible for everyone to sample the variety.

**Liqueur Sampling**—To warm up guests on a nippy winter night, ask them to bring their favorite bottle of liqueur for a "Liqueur Sampling." Serve coffee drinks laced with liqueur, hot wine or hot cider. This idea is also good for a neighborhood gathering since no one has to drive home after an evening of "tasting." Remember to offer non-alcoholic beverages, too.

**Charity Begins at Home**—Another "admission" for your Winterfest could be that guests bring items for a charitable organization. In winter months, charities are usually more needy. So while you are gathered together in a warm, cozy house, remember the people in the community who aren't so lucky. Host a food or clothing drive based on one of these categories:

- food items for the homeless (or blankets, gloves, used clothing)
- lunch bags for a food shelter filled with sandwiches, fruit, snacks, and a drink box (deliver promptly the following day)
- baby items for a pregnancy center such as diapers, wipes, blankets, formula, baby food, juice, powder, bibs, and T-shirts

**Activity Swap**—You can also "swap" with each other. Admission could be items related to things we do to keep busy during the cold months. Ask guests to bring novels, cds, puzzles, or movie videos to trade.

## Winter White Food Suggestions

In keeping with the nature of "a white winter," plan a co-op dinner and have each neighbor bring a contribution of "white" food. For instance, someone brings a few bottles of white wine and someone else brings a loaf of white bread. Make sure all the components of the meal are included: main dish, salads, starches, vegetables. Here is a list of possibilities for white food. Have fun inventing others!

| | |
|---|---|
| rice | New England clam chowder |
| mashed potatoes | white meat of chicken or turkey |
| macaroni dishes | marshmallows |
| cauliflower | vanilla ice cream |
| potato salad | snowballs |
| potato soup | coconut cake with white icing |

## Games & Contests

**Frozen T-Shirt Contest**—A few days before the party, roll or fold a bunch of wet T-shirts and put them in the freezer. Teams must undo the T-shirt by whatever means possible. The first team to have a member put on the shirt wins.

**Luge Liqueur Race**—Have a giant block of ice delivered. On the deck, driveway or in the yard, set up the block so it is on a 45 degree angle. Drill or use a blow torch to create one or more "luge" courses in the ice. Then pour a shot of liqueur at the top, letting it roll through

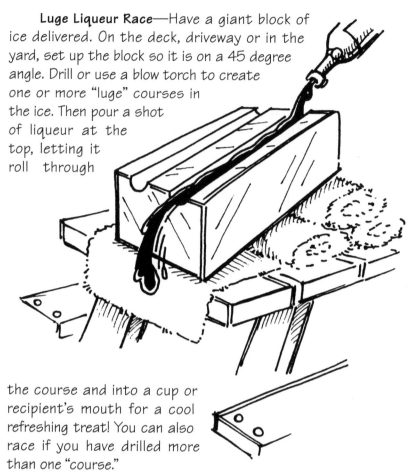

the course and into a cup or recipient's mouth for a cool refreshing treat! You can also race if you have drilled more than one "course."

**Winter Clothes Relay**—Provide two piles of winter clothing including scarves, large size boots, ski pants, coats, mittens, and hats. Make two teams. The first person on each team runs to the pile of clothes and dresses in all of them as fast as possible. S/he then takes off the clothes, runs to the back of the line, and the second person begins dressing. Each team member has to dress and undress as quickly as possible. The team who finishes first wins.

**Games**—Entertain the group with board games, charades or cards.

# February's Sweethearts' Supper

## A sit-down dinner for your favorite "cupid couples"

Cupid has struck! Hold this amorous dinner party during the week of Valentine's Day by inviting married couples and established sweethearts. A dozen people is cozy and manageable, especially if you are the chef.

## Invitation Ideas

**Hearts or Lips**—Print the party details from the computer onto heart laser paper. Or, write your invitation on puckered lip shapes made out of red construction paper. Address pink envelopes with a red calligraphy marker, and decorate envelopes with cherub or heart stickers, or an angel rubber stamp.

**Bring a poem**—Ask each guest to write a poem to their significant other before the party, then invite them to bring along the poems. Before dinner, go around the table and have each guest read their poem to their partner. Laughter and tears will abound!

## Party Favors

**A Spoonful**—Buy chocolate spoons and place a chocolate kiss on each. Wrap in pink plastic wrap or tissue paper, and tie together with pink or white ribbon. Attach a tag which reads, "a spoonful of love."

**For Her**—At each woman's place setting, put a small red gift bag filled with a refrigerator magnet with a love theme, cherub soap, or a heart or angel gift. Also include candy hearts. Put heart or cherub stickers on the bag.

**For Him**—At each man's place setting, place a love poem. Print the poem from the computer and glue it to red construction paper to make a tent card. Write the poem yourself or feel free to use this poem, written by the author with her husband in mind, for her Sweethearts' Supper.

### In Your Eyes

*I have the look of love tonight
As I peer into your eyes,
The thrill I feel each time I look
Always takes me by surprise.*

*I see reflected back to me,
Your love and faith and trust.
A loving bond between us that
No time will ever rust.*

*In your eyes I see just why
We attracted from the start.
You stole my soul, my being,
Especially my heart.*

*More often I should speak these words,
You will always be the one.
My life, my mate, for now and then,
It is my love that you have won.*

*Suzanne Singleton
February, 1994*

## Placecards

Take instant pictures of the couples as they arrive. Use as placecards or frame them to give as party favors. Or, make red and white placecards with heart stickers on card stock (available in office supply and craft stores).

# Decorations

**Big Hearts**—Make large red hearts from construction paper or poster board, and write each couple's name on a heart. Decorate the hearts with cupid rubber stamps or stickers. Tape the hearts to the wall in the dining area.

**On the Table**—Use a red tablecloth, heart napkins, and red, pink and white balloons. Sprinkle candy hearts or red hot cinnamon hearts all over the table.

**Love Cake**—Make a heart cake, or decorate a cake with candy hearts.

**Lots of Angels**—Decorate with lots of angel figurines all around the dining area. Use an angel centerpiece, angel candlesticks and angel napkin rings.

**Cupid Strikes**—Hire someone to surprise your guests by arriving as "Cupid"—bow and arrow included! Or, maybe your spouse would volunteer to dress up in costume (homemade red diaper, short curly wig, red lipstick, heart tattoo, angel wings, bow and arrow).

# Games

**The Sweetheart's Game** (for adults only!)—In a bowl, place folded pieces of paper containing the following questions and instructions. Pass the bowl around the table and have each couple pick a paper and respond to what it says. Some questions and commands are corny, some are romantic, some are a bit racy! Make up a few of your own, too.

- Tell your partner why you are happy that you married him/her.
- Recite a few words of love from a famous poem.
- Sing a song with your partner that contains the word 'love' or 'angel.'
- Name a birthmark, mole or spot on your partner's body that is hidden.

- What is the pet name you use as a couple to refer to a man's "jewels?"
- What is the pet name you use as a couple to refer to a woman's chest?
- What is your nickname for each other?
- What animal's feet does your partner's feet resemble?
- Give your partner a French kiss.
- What is the most unusual place you have ever made love?
- Make a loving toast to your sweetheart.
- What is your favorite part of your partner's body?
- Hold hands with your partner and lock eyes for one full minute.
- Name a place outside of the home where you fantasize about making love.
- Look into your partner's eyes and tell him/her three things that you absolutely love about him/her.

**More Love Games**—There are also a few board games on the market like "Scruples," "The Dating Game," or "The Newlywed Game" which would fit this party theme and be fun to play as a group.

## Lip Smackin' Competition

Give the ladies a small piece of paper and a tube of bright lipstick. Each has to kiss the paper, leaving the best lip print possible. Then they must name their kisses, like "Luscious Lips" or "Kiss Me Baby." Ask the men to judge the contest by selecting the best pair of lips, and naming second and first runners-up.

## The Flip Side

Maybe you are not feeling so amorous this month after recently divorcing. Throw a "Divorced The Deadbeat" or "Divorced The Diphead" party! Why not? You celebrated when you were married, why not celebrate moving on with your life?

# March's Peekin' at the Past Picture Party

### A trip down memory lane

If you're like most people, you have boxes and boxes stuffed with pictures of your life. Realistically, how many of your friends and family have ever had the opportunity to see them?

Here's a simple excuse to gather a group of family or friends together. Host a picture party! This works better if the group has a common thread, like a group of high school friends, cousins, current or past co-workers, or a group who hasn't seen each other in a while. Have everyone bring photos reminiscent of the time you shared together. Make an assembly line or organized setup to share the pictures with each other so everyone can benefit from viewing. Remember to take pictures of this party as you create a new memory!

## Decorations

**Picture Posters**—Inexpensively enough, negatives of your favorite pictures can be enlarged to poster size to hang around the room. If you have a bunch of pictures framed of the people who are coming to the party, set them around the party area, too.

**Collage of Photos**—Have each guest contribute a few pictures prior to the party for you to create a large collage as a decoration. Make the collage on a large piece of poster board with photos of all sizes. This can be then given away later at the party as a prize.

## Favors

Give away photo albums, disposable cameras, film and picture frames as favors or prizes. You can also include prepaid phone cards, and stationary and stamps to help guests keep in touch.

## Picture Contests

**Categories**—Announce in your invitation that guests should bring pictures to enter in a photo contest using the following categories: funniest,

classic, oldest, sexiest, silliest, most emotional, ugliest, and most beautiful. Set up and number the photos as the guests arrive, then later have everyone vote on a piece of paper.

**Bouncing Babies**—Have everyone bring a baby picture of themselves. Post these on a large poster board and number them. Guests have to speculate who is who. Award a prize to the person who most correctly matched pictures to people.

## More Memories

**More to See**—Have guests also bring scrapbooks, home movies, yearbooks, and memory boxes.

**Slide Show**—Have everyone send you ten or so slides before the party for you to create a slide show. If someone does not own slides, photos can be easily made into slides using the negatives. This will take some time, so plan accordingly.

# April's Surprise Golf Tournament

## A day on the links and an after-golf party

(This event references "husband" for ease of writing.)

Here is a special and great golf day "fore" the golfer in your life! Plan a surprise golf tournament at your country club or public golf course. Arrange this golf outing with the golf course manager to assure tee times for the date of your choice. A Saturday or Sunday morning would work best, although keep in mind that golf courses are most crowded on weekends. You can try a morning during the week, keeping in mind that some guests may find it difficult to fit the tournament into their work schedules. You'll have better chances of participation if you give guests plenty of notice.

## Planning

Make tee times for groups of four consisting of your husband's friends. You may want to invite a few old friends whom your husband has not seen in a while. Think of former work friends, school friends and golf buddies.

Invite each guest to arrive about 30 minutes before your husband. To get him there without suspicion, have one of his friends invite him to play a round of golf, or you can invite him if you ordinarily golf together.

## Tee Off

Surprise him with everyone in the clubhouse at a continental breakfast, keeping it simple and quick so golfers can begin on time. Maybe you can bring in your own supply of donuts, danish, bagels and cream cheese, croissants, juices, and coffee. Or, you may want the guests to order from the breakfast menu. Breakfast depends on your budget, time constraints and the choices offered by the clubhouse.

If it is easier to obtain tee time in the afternoon, start with a luncheon. This scheduling will work better anyway if you decide to also host an after-golf party. (See Post-Golf Fun below.)

## Contests

The golf course manager can help you create contests for the tournament. For instance, some of the standard ones are "closest to the pin," "least amount of putts," and "longest drive." The best "par" per group is the winner of the tournament.

## Prizes

After the tournament, have an awards presentation. Golf related gifts will work well, such as golf towels, sleeves of balls, tees, and golf accessories. Maybe the winning foursome can receive a certificate to play a round of golf at the same course, or a gift certificate to the pro shop. Negotiate with the golf course manager to donate the certificates since

you are patronizing the golf course with your event.

## Post-Golf Fun

After the tournament, invite the golfers back to your house (or host a party at the clubhouse) where you will surprise your husband with a second party. Unbeknownst to him, he will bid goodbye to his friends, not knowing that they are continuing the celebration. The second party will include wives, girlfriends, and non-golfing friends to complete the guest list . . . and the party continues!

# May's
# Triple Crown Infield Party

### Enjoy horse racing from your own backyard

**E**ach racetrack involved in the Triple Crown—Churchill Downs in Louisville, Kentucky (Kentucky Derby); Pimlico Race Course in Baltimore, Maryland (Preakness Stakes); and Belmont Park in Elmont, New York (Belmont Stakes)—allows the public to buy tickets to the infield, where an enormous party is held with massive numbers of people. If you have ever been to one of these infield parties, you have battled the crowds, staked your claim on the lawn, and sweltered in the sun all day while the races happened around you. To avoid actually attending an infield party while staying in the spirit of The Triple Crown, host your own infield party!

You will need a large yard to accommodate guests. As if they were attending the actual infield party, everyone brings their own food, chairs, blankets, coolers, and beverages. You provide trash cans, a port-a-pot (if you don't want your house open), games, and a TV to watch the races.

Remember to send press releases to local TV stations and newspapers to see if they will cover your "event." Your party guests will love hamming it up for the cameras and this party will be the talk of the year!

## Decorations

**Flowers**—Order a horseshoe of flowers on a stand from a florist.

**Jerseys**—Hang jockey silks from the deck or fence which are cut out rectangles of silky, colorful fabric.

**Big Banner**—Hang a banner reading "Welcome to the Infield!"

**Props**—If you live in Baltimore, Louisville or New York, contact the racetrack and ask for any extra props or decorations like T-shirts, buttons, pins or posters.

**Track**—Make an oval area around the infield to simulate the racecourse by drawing on the grass with white spray paint. Make a START and FINISH line.

**Program**—Just for fun, make up a program booklet using guests' names as horses' names, such as 'Stuart Oh Baby' or 'Alicia Alive' and print odds on each.

## Games

**Horseshoes**—Set up a game of horseshoes (far from party area for safety). You may also want to set up a volleyball court or badminton area for additional activities.

**Horse Races**—Rent a horse racing game like you see at carnivals. (Look up Party Planning or Party Supply Rentals in the yellow pages.)

**Horse Relay**—Have a horse relay using toy stick horses. Teams gallop from the "starting gate" to the "finish line" and back again, handing off the stick horse and a jersey to the next contestant. (Make rectangular jerseys out of silky and colorful fabric with a head hole cut out in the center.) The team who finishes first wins.

**Betting**—Bet on the real races with play money. People then cash in their winnings for prizes such as store and restaurant gift certificates. Ask for donations from local establishments—it's a good promotion for them. Or, you can take bets on the final horse race of the day by making a "pool." Write the horses' names and post positions down the left side of a poster board. Across the top, write WIN, PLACE and SHOW. People purchase the squares for whatever horse they think may win. The total money collected is then split 50-25-25 (WIN-PLACE-SHOW) between the guests who chose the winning horses.

# June's
# Around the Globe

## Experiencing other cultures

This party is a good opportunity to travel to other countries without leaving your living room! It is also a chance to celebrate ethnic backgrounds and to taste foods from around the globe. On the invitation, ask guests to select a country to represent. They may want to select the country of their family origin. When guests respond, keep a list of the country they will be representing to prevent duplication. Guests may want to dress in costume indicative of the selected country.

## Invitations

Make your invitation look like a passport, an airline ticket, a globe, or make it into a paper airplane. You can also print it on white paper and paste it to a piece of a map. Or, ask an airline ticket counter for a bunch of "folders" which tickets are placed into for travel, and send

invitations inside of those, also placing them into envelopes to mail. Another idea is to place your invitations inside of "air mail" envelopes, then place them inside of regular envelopes so as not to confuse the post office.

# Food

**Potpourri**—Guests bring a dish representing a food from the selected country. Tell everyone the number of people expected so guests know how much food to bring.

**What is it?**—Make tent cards identifying the food (and its ingredients) on the buffet. This is so people know what they are eating, and to protect someone who may be allergic to a specific ingredient.

**On the Bar**—Include imported beers and wines.

# Decorations

**Souvenirs**—When you know which countries are going to be represented, hunt around for souvenirs and items from that country to use as decorations. Scan the library for books and music, and ask your friends what they have to lend: dolls, clothes, costumes, books, knickknacks, products, pictures, and posters.

**Pretty Pictures**—Ask a travel agency for various posters and brochures—hang the posters and scatter the brochures around the serving table. Blow up photos from previous overseas trips.

**On the Table**—As a tablecloth, use real maps, or select fabric of a globe design, or an ethnic design (i.e. red and white checkered for Italian).

**Festive Flags**—Hang international flags around the party room. You can make these easily from colored poster board. Or, look in a party store for a string of flags.

**In the Powder Room**—Hang posters and maps of the world in the bathroom for people to study. Also, guests will get a kick out of listening to a language lesson on audiotape while using the facilities.

**And more**—Hang a pinata. Set out a globe and an atlas.

## Games

**Globe Spin**—Provide a globe. Game coordinator spins the globe. Contestant yells stop at any time. Game coordinator stops the globe with one finger that will be pointing to a country or body of water. Participant must name the body of water (without getting close enough to read it), or name a city in the country where the finger is pointing. This can be played in teams.

**Trivia**—Make up a trivia game using geography books, or use the geography questions from a trivia game.

## Variations

If you and your friends have planned a trip to another country, host this party either *before* your trip to get everyone into the spirit, or *after* your trip so everyone can relive the vacation through pictures, food and souvenirs (have them bring what they bought).

Plan this same theme for a group such as a school, an organization, a senior center, or as a learning experience for children.

# July's Casino Bus Trip

## A full day of fun on a busy bus and at the casino

This is a great idea for an inexpensive party on wheels! This idea works well as a surprise party for someone's retirement, anniversary or birthday. Although you can pick any destination for your bus trip, the ideas presented here are casino-related.

Organize a trip to a casino through a local bus company. Send flyers to the guests, inviting more people than the actual number of seats on the bus (not everyone will be able to attend). For instance, if the bus holds 45 people, send about 65 invitations.

Guests respond by sending a check for the cost of the bus trip. Don't worry about asking people to pay their own way since most casinos hand out vouchers worth equal value of the bus ticket.

## Invitations

Design a flyer with the bus trip information: cost, destination, reason for the party, date, time, place to meet, response information. Print your flyer on festive laser paper which you can easily find in office supply stores or use casino related graphics to spice up the flyer. Allow ample time for people to return checks.

Include in the envelope a few poker chips, a few playing cards or fake money to spark people's interest in attending. Indicate that it is a SURPRISE so that no one snitches to the guest of honor.

# On the Bus

**When to Meet**—Have the guest of honor arrive 30 minutes later than everyone else to assure that your guests will be there to greet him/her when s/he boards the bus.

**Coin Rolls**—Instead of everyone bringing a gift, ask for rolls of quarters and nickels. Place these in a gift bag for the guest of honor. Make a gigantic card for everyone to sign.

**A Roast**—Ask a few people (whom are good speakers and witty) to give a short speech or prepare an anecdote, then "roast" the guest of honor.

**Say What?**—Pass around a blank journal with a pen and encourage each guest to write a message of congratulations to the person being honored.

**Just for Fun**—Print T-shirts, buttons or hats with the person's or couple's name(s) and special occasion. Be sure to include the date and trip destination.

**Bus Decor**—Decorate the inside of the bus with occasion-related decor: retirement signs, birthday banners, streamers, balloons, photos, etc.

**Treat on the Seat**—Provide a breakfast treat on each seat of the bus in a colored lunch bag: a styrofoam coffee cup (have insulated containers of coffee available), muffin or donut, fruit, toaster pastry, and a juice box. For the return trip, provide coolers of soda and/or beer (check with the bus company on alcohol policy) and light snacks such as pretzels and popcorn. Buy individual snack bags and hand out as guests get back on the bus.

## Games

**Bad Joke**—Have a contest for telling the worst and best jokes.

**Top Ten**—Make up a "Top Ten Reason" list about the guest of honor.

**Try Trivia**—Make up a trivia game about the guest of honor. People write down their answers as you read each question. The person who knows the most answers wins.

# August's Hen Pecks

### *Girls get together*

## Big Girls Slumber Party

When was the last time you attended a slumber party, not counting your own daughter's? How fun to gather together a group of adult girlfriends and have an entire night to giggle, drink wine, relax and stay up half the night. (Kids, husbands and pets must be cleared out of the house!) Invite everyone to bring their pillows, sleeping bags, and favorite stuffed animals. Send the invitation in a toothbrush holder.

**Pamper**—Hire a manicurist, a masseuse or a hair stylist. Or, style each other's hair and paint each other's toe- and finger-nails.

**More Fun**—Watch old movies and play old music from high school days. Play games. Gab. Share. And of course, wear your pajamas!

**Slipper Parade**—Have a slipper parade. Each friend models a pair of slippers for the "judges." Select the ugliest, oldest, cutest, prettiest, and funniest. Also judge the cutest, ugliest, prettiest, and funniest feet and toes!

**Well-loved**—See who brought the oldest, most well-loved stuffed animal from childhood.

**Talented Tootsies**—Have a contest to see who can draw the best picture on paper with their toes.

## Crafty Creatures

Share your talent while enjoying time with a group of friends. Teach them your creative specialty, or bring in another person to demonstrate ceramics, pottery, jewelry, holiday crafts, wreaths, flower arranging, cake decorating, stenciling, basket weaving, or applying makeup. Provide all of the materials needed.

## Shopping Excursions

Plan a day of outlet shopping with your friends where you can enjoy each other's friendship for a full day, do not have to answer to "Mommy," lunch at your leisure, shop slowly, and take a day for yourself. Traveling there together on a bus or in a van is half the fun!

## Mothers & Daughters Unite

This idea works well with your girls' group or high school friends and your moms. Plan a breakfast, brunch, luncheon, dinner, or tea at someone's house or a private room in a restaurant. The daughters treat their moms to the meal.

**Sharing**—Have each mom share a growing up anecdote about the daughter.

**Show & Tell**—Have each daughter "show and tell" about a very special gift or memento which the mother has given the daughter sometime in her life.

**Who's Who?**—Ask everyone to bring a baby picture of themselves. Number them and display on a large poster board. The object is to match pictures with people. The winner who guesses the most correctly wins a favor.

**Sweet Poetry**—Write a sweet poem about motherhood. Print it on pretty paper, frame it, then give as favors to the moms. Feel free to use this poem, written by the author for her mom, for a Mother/Daughter Girls' Night.

### Happy Mother's Day, Mom!

*On the day of my birth we bonded,
My life you gave to me.
You held my tiny hand,
Promising what was to be.*

*You fed me and you clothed me,
You taught me wrong from right.
You nursed me and you held me,
When I was sick throughout the night.*

*You sang silly words and played,
In the years when I was little,
Then guided me through changes,
During the years in the middle.*

*While working hard, you still spared time
To teach, support, advise.
You raised me to be a woman,
And the pride shows in your eyes.*

*Motherhood is such a challenge,
A tough job without any pay.
Yet some reward must exist,
As you continue to mother each day.*

*Now I know the reward is love,
Between little girl and mother.
A special love, a life-long bond,
So unlike any other.*

*"Thanks" could never say enough
For all you've done through my days.
So please accept these heartfelt words,
Of pride, of love, of praise.*

*Suzanne Singleton
May 1996*

# September's Vacation's Over

### Vacationers reunite to share videos, pictures and memories

Returning from vacation is coming back to reality, and sometimes, it can be a bit of a letdown. Most likely you had a great time, enjoyed the people who were with you, laughed and relaxed. Keep the trip alive by hosting a Vacation's Over party.

## Invitations

Simply write the party details on the back of a photo from the vacation, and mail it like a postcard. Invite the group who were on your vacation and ask them to bring their pictures and videos from the trip and any souvenirs that they bought.

## Decor

Recreate the vacation's theme. If it was a beach vacation, invite friends dressed in beach attire, set up beach umbrellas, coolers, and beach chairs. On the floor, lay out beach towels and toys along with a few buckets of sand. Play an audiotape of crashing waves and cawing seagulls.

## Party Game

**Taboo**—Pass out three plastic Hawaiian leis to everyone. Select two taboo words relating to the vacation (like "beach" and "Hawaii"). Any time someone says these words to another, a lei is taken from the guest who said it. The person with the most leis at the end of the party wins a prize. Substitute the lei for something else related to the vacation, such as tees for a golf vacation or clothespins for a camping vacation.

# October's
# One Costume Halloween Party

## Guests dress up as the same character or theme

For a unique twist to a Halloween party, invite everyone dressed as the same character or group. Instead of decorating in traditional Halloween decor of spider webs, blood, and pumpkins, decorate in the character's theme. Choose from these ideas . . .

- Super Heroes: Superman, Spiderman, Batman, Wonder Woman, Mighty Mouse
- TV show characters: M.A.S.H., Simpsons, Flintstones, Gilligan's Island, Seinfeld
- Marilyn Monroe
- Elvis
- Groucho Marx or the Marx Brothers
- nerds
- celebrities or sports figures
- deceased celebrities
- Disney characters
- Wizard of Oz characters
- circus performers
- monsters
- products and objects
- nursery rhymes or fairy tales
- cartoons
- movies
- hobbies
- cross-dressing (men as women, women as men)
- fad of the year
- the Beatles or other musical group

## Costume of the Month

Another Halloween party idea is to assign guests a month of the year and ask them to dress in costume pertaining to that month's theme or holiday, such as:

January . . . . . . . . . . . . Winter or President's Day
February . . . . . . . . . . . . Valentine's Day
March . . . . . . . . . . . . . . St. Patrick's Day
April . . . . . . . . . . . . . . . Easter or Passover
May . . . . . . . . . . . . . . . Spring or Memorial Day
June . . . . . . . . . . . . . . . Summer
July . . . . . . . . . . . . . . . Independence Day
August . . . . . . . . . . . . . Tourist Season
September . . . . . . . . . . Fall or Back to School
October . . . . . . . . . . . . Halloween
November . . . . . . . . . . . Thanksgiving
December . . . . . . . . . . Christmas, Hanukkah or Kwaanza

# November's
# Gift 'n Gab Gathering

## A gift and craft show in your home

This event kicks off the holiday shopping season in a low-stress way, and is a good excuse to gather together a group of girls for a night of gab! Host it on the day after Thanksgiving—"Black Friday"— the busiest shopping day of the year. Plan it in the evening so as not to interfere with people's plans during the day, since most adults and kids have off from work and school. Make this a "girls only" party and indicate that it will be "child-free."

Invite about six "vendors" to your home to display merchandise. Maybe you know someone who wrote a book, owns a retail store, or makes doll clothes or holiday crafts. You will be surprised at how many people have wares to sell. A sample list of vendors may look like this:

- retailer—to sell store inventory, such as from an angel store
- jeweler—to sell handmade jewelry and accept custom jewelry orders
- crafter—to sell handmade holiday crafts, pins, boxes and sweatshirts
- publisher—to sell books, cards, journals, bookmarks, and gift baskets
- photographer—to sell framed photos and photo greeting cards
- author—to sell books

## Planning

Decide on an early evening starting time and make it an open house so that guests will arrive at various times without overwhelming the vendors. Name an ending time so people know up to what time they can arrive, or leave it open ended to give it more of a party feel.

## Invitation

A flyer works well because it provides the needed space to describe the event. Use gift package graphics across the top. Describe each of your vendors and merchandise to be displayed. If you need a head count to plan the food, include an RSVP number, and of course, directions to your house. Invite more guests than you actually want—not everyone will show. Perhaps each vendor could supply a list of customers to invite. Vendors share the cost of mailing the flyers.

    **Extra Friend**—Ask guests to bring an extra friend to add to the guest list. Some people do not like to attend parties alone, especially where they may not know anyone.

    **Door Prizes**—Mention on the flyer that door prizes will be presented. Ask each vendor to donate one or two items.

## Arrival

To prevent yourself from having to constantly answer the door in this open house setting, post a colorful sign at the entrance that indicates guests should walk in. Set up a tray table inside the foyer with a small tent card instructing them to make a name tag and grab a drink. Indicate where to place coats.

## Name tags

Most likely, not all of your girlfriends will know everyone, so it's perfectly fine to provide name tags (put markers and tags on the tray table near the front door). People appreciate knowing with whom they are chatting. It becomes easier to make a new friend when you know her name. A name tag can also include a quick fact about the person such as a few hobbies, number of children, maiden name, etc. to help start conversation.

## Refreshments

Serve wine, wine coolers, champagne punch and an assortment of soft drinks. Have each vendor bring two appetizers or snack-type foods.

## Vendor Setup

Stagger vendors throughout your house, perhaps two to a room. This keeps people flowing throughout the space instead of congregating in one area. Reserve the kitchen for refreshments and food. Clear away knickknacks and clutter and use your tables and furniture to display the items.

## Vendor Payment

Have a common cash register (ask someone to be the cashier) or ask each vendor to collect payment for whatever they sell. The advantage of having a common cash register is that guests do not have to pull out their wallets or write checks multiple times. Be sure to code each item with the vendor's initials to keep accurate accounting. Write each vendor a check for their sales after the event is over.

If the vendors accept credit cards, have them supply a pile of charge receipts to the cashier.

## Decorations

If you have the energy to decorate your home for Christmas for this event, it will certainly add a festive feeling to the evening. You may want to hang white Christmas lights, or burn incense, potpourri or candles to add pleasant scents to your home.

# December's
# Holiday Caroling Bonfire

## Good old fashioned singing around the campfire

This is an easy, no-fuss party. It can be a spur of the moment gathering since it involves little planning and no cooking.

This party should be held in a large yard where it is safe to build a fire. Follow campfire guidelines for fire safety. A rain date should be selected. Invite neighbors, friends and family with their lawn chairs for a relaxing evening of singing around the campfire to boost holiday spirits and take a breather from the bustle of the holiday season. This is a good way for neighbors to group together to better acquaint with each other. Remember to invite the new neighbors, too!

No need to bother with food. A tray of cookies and hot chocolate will suffice. Invite guests to bring a thermos full of their favorite warmer-upper!

Provide song sheets. Invite a guitarist to help with the music.

# Rough Sketch Ideas . . . More Adult Themes

## Beatles Bash

No matter how much time has passed since The Beatles were on the charts and the craze of the music world, people will always remember and love them. For that group of friends who just can't forget, plan a Beatles Bash! Have everyone dress up like one of the Beatles, play Beatles music, and decorate with Beatles posters and albums. Watch a Beatles concert on tape, and scream a lot!

## Chinese New Year

Hang Chinese paper lanterns, throw on a kimono and you're ready to celebrate the Chinese New Year, or Yuan Tan, which falls between January 21 and February 19th. Your party doesn't have to last two weeks like the ones in China, but make it a good one as you serve various dishes of Chinese food: soups, stir fry, chicken and beef, and noodle dishes. Make a small tray of dipping sauces with hot mustard, soy sauce, and duck sauce. Demonstrate how to use chopsticks. Serve various teas, and remember the fortune cookies!

## The Envelope Please

It's too bad that most Hollywood-related award programs are aired during the week, because watching them makes a great reason to gather a group of friends. You could plan a party to watch music, movie or TV awards (Emmys, Oscars, Grammys, etc.) by taping the desired show and hosting your party on a weekend. Ask your guests to hold off watching the program until the party, so everyone can predict the winners and enjoy the outcome. Give out movie passes or music store certificates as door prizes.

## Fairy Godmother Party

Let your kids do the party planning for a special "Fairy Godmother" in their lives. Maybe she's an aunt, a babysitter, daycare provider, neighbor, nanny, or "other" mother. Let kids plan the menu and play games of their choice. Ask them to produce a puppet show to tell a story of how they feel about this special person. Have them make cards and gifts. Give the Fairy Godmother a magic wand and a halo of stars at this celebration in her honor!

## Game Night

Your guests will be "game" to play at this party! Dust off your favorite games and let the fun begin! There are a slew of fun adult games on the market like 'Mad Gab,' 'L-C-R Dice,' 'Taboo,' 'Oodles,' 'Balderdash,' 'Pictionary,' and lots more. Play the same game every time or alternate each month. Friends in the group can take turns hosting it, and there's no fuss for one person to make food because "admission" for everyone is to bring one easy snack: chip and dip, baked pretzels, veggies and dip, nachos and salsa, peanuts, etc. The hostess can provide beverages.

## Guest of Honor Look-a-like

This party is a comical way to honor a friend or family member, especially one with a sense of humor who is a character himself! If the party is to honor Uncle Louie, then invite the guests to come dressed up as an Uncle Louie look-a-like! Dressing up ideas include imitating hobbies indicative of the guest of honor, wearing specific clothes the person prefers, a trademark the person is known for, or a physical trait such as bushy white eyebrows. This is guaranteed to spice up the party and provide instant laughter when you see how creative people can be!

## Here She Comes, Miss America!

Beauty pageants are usually aired on a "school night" which makes it difficult to get together with a bunch of friends to enjoy them. To watch the Miss USA or Miss Universe pageant, tape the show and host this party the following weekend. Again, ask your friends not to watch the show. When guests respond to the invitation, ask for their predictions of the winner and runners-up before the program is aired. Provide sashes and tiaras for everyone—yes, even the guys! Set up a panel of judges. The person who predicted the winner receives a bunch of roses and a fake diamond tiara and must walk down a pretend runway while everyone sings, "Here She Comes, Miss America!"

## Holiday Pitch-In

For some, the hardest part about hosting a holiday party may be the cooking and the financing. Why do it all? If you would like to invite the entire clan for Easter, Thanksgiving, or Christmas, but would rather not be responsible for all the work and the budget, delegate! Make it a holiday pitch-in party.

Decide on the menu and assign each family member a dish: someone brings the turkey, someone else brings the sweet potatoes, two people bring desserts, etc. You supply the chairs, tables, paper goods and ice. Charge "admission" of one or two food items, two liters of soda, and a six pack of beer or a bottle of wine.

This idea works well also by renting an inexpensive hall. Check with small churches, schools, VFW or Kiwanis halls, local clubs, apartment complexes, etc. Each family pitches in a share of the rental fee. Divvy up the supplies and food: one family brings cups, another brings plates, a third brings ice, etc. Tables and chairs most likely are included with the hall. Remember to bring a television for the football fans. Bring board games and card games to play as a group. Keep the children busy with crafts and have someone bring a small TV/VCR combo to play kids' movies.

## Mardi Gras Fest

Just like in the French Quarters of New Orleans, Louisiana, it's Mardi Gras time at your quarters! Celebrate the spirit of this spring festival by wearing half masks, gaudy and sprightly costumes, and lots of feathers! Trade beaded necklaces with each other. Serve cajun food like blackened chicken, fish or shrimp, sausage, crawfish, and of course, jumbalaya (rice, chicken and sausage). Bury a small toy baby doll in a "King Cake" which is a round coffee cake with a hole in the center, decorated with green, purple and gold icing. Whoever eats the piece of cake with the baby in it is committed to throwing the next party!

## Marriage Memories

For better or worse, for richer or poorer, in sickness and in health . . . and at parties! Invite couples to celebrate anniversaries or reminisce about their wedding days. Ask them to dress in their wedding gowns and tuxedos that they actually wore (if they still fit! If not, just bring them). Ask them also to bring wedding albums to share with the group. Order a small wedding cake and let couples feed each other, toast with champagne, throw garters and bouquets, slow dance, maybe even renew their vows!

## Meet the Graduate

Here's a terrific way to surprise and congratulate a friend or family member who is ready to graduate. Meet the person outside of the building after his or her last school exam. Bring along a party of friends, a picnic basket, and champagne or sparkling cider to celebrate the end of studying with a picnic on the grass! The student will be surprised and have the opportunity to unwind and celebrate freedom from school!

## Milestone Plus One

If you know that your spouse is expecting a party for his 50th birthday, confuse him by not giving him one! Instead, plan a FIFTY PLUS ONE party for the following year for a guaranteed surprise. Or, do the opposite and plan a 49th birthday party about a week after his birthday and call it an "ALMOST 50" celebration (or "PUSHING 50," "THE YEAR BEFORE 50," "355 DAYS UNTIL 50.") You get the idea, and he'll get quite a surprise!

## Movie Night

Unwind with a group of friends while you go to the movies in your own living room! Rent a popular movie or order a pay-per-view and serve popcorn in fun clown bags, and popular movie candy such as licorice (see licorice tray idea on page 169), chocolate covered raisins, and gummy bears. This kind of casual party is also one which you can plan monthly, taking turns at each other's homes.

## New Home Christening

Buying a new home is an important event in your family's life and should be recognized accordingly! So have a ribbon cutting ceremony with a bunch of friends outside of your new house. Serve champagne, take photos, set a "family garden stone" in the yard (i.e., Singletons, settled May 1999), then go inside for more celebrating!

## Scavenger Hunt

Kids aren't the only ones who would enjoy a scavenger hunt. Adults can have one too! Invite guests to meet at your house at a designated time. Everyone brings a food dish to share. Teams are decided beforehand and a team name is selected before leaving for the hunt. All cars leave the party site at the same time. Teams are told what to bring to help them figure out clues: a Bible, phone book, instant camera, dictionary, a pad of paper and a pen, and maps—whatever you suggest that might help them with the clues.

Ahead of time, you will have placed various clues all over town on index cards in store windows, on signs, near driveway entrances, etc. Teams are allowed to call in for hints. Hand out sheets with the rules of the hunt, mandatory pictures to take, items to bring back, and the first clue. The first team back with the required items is the winner. Place a time limit on the scavenger hunt so everyone makes it back to your house for the post-hunt party.

For more detailed ideas to plan this scavenger hunt, see Mall Quest on page 114 in the Teen Time chapter.

## Sports of Sorts

Worldly sporting events are big time nowadays, with lots of pomp and hoopla, and certainly these events are covered heavily by our media. Host a party around whatever sports event is happening in the world which interests you and your friends, and cheer on your favorite team, player or country! Some to choose from:

| | |
|---|---|
| Wimbledon | US Open |
| Daytona 500 | All-Star Game |
| World Series | Super Bowl (first do a tailgate party) |
| Stanley Cup | British Open |
| PGA Championship | The Masters |
| World Cup | Triple Crown |
| Summer Olympics | Winter Olympics |

## Swap Meet

It's easy to get bored with our belongings. So here is a chance to get rid of gently used "stuff" that is collecting in your basement, garage, and other cluttered rooms. Plan a "swap meet" with your neighbors. You can name it specifically, like "Toy Swap" or "Music Swap," where everyone trades only items of the same nature. Or, make it a generic swap, inviting everyone to bring clothes, books, small electronics, exercise equipment, kids' clothes, toys, videos, music, gadgets, exercise tapes, etc. You may be sick of listening to the same 20 compact disks, so why not trade them with someone else who has a different musical selection? None of your kids ever jump on that mini trampoline, so trade it for a badminton set which may excite your children for a while. Get the idea? Meet . . . and swap! Remember, one person's reject is another's treasure!

## Sixties and Seventies

Pull out those old clothes or visit thrift shops to outfit yourself in the days of past. Who knows, you may just have a few clothes which you are "saving" for when they come back in style! Select a decade and invite your guests to join in the fun of remembering what it was like back then.

## Winter White Fun

Host an ice skating party at a shallow pond if you have one near your property. Ice skate, build a bonfire, roast marshmallows, sip hot chocolate and munch on snacks. If snow is available, have a snowman building or snow sculpting contest, or race on snow tubes, toboggans or sleds.

# Tips for Adult Parties

## *If you are the Hostess . . .*

**Invitations**—Computer programs with graphics and various fonts provide an easy way to create customized party invitations. Office supply and craft stores sell all-occasion festive paper and matching envelopes for laser printing.

**Envelopes**—Brighten up invitation envelopes using colored markers, rubber stamps, stickers, and pretty postage. Write the addresses on the envelopes for a more personal touch. If you do not have neat handwriting, ask someone to address the envelopes for you. Match the envelopes with a color in the invitation.

**What to Say**—Use colorful language instead of the standard "You are invited to. . . ." Call it "Breakfast with the Bride" or "Thanksgiving Family Feast." Instead of using the word "party," give your event a creative name like "Superbowl Sizzler" or "Girls' Gabby Gathering."

**What About Kids?**—If children are not invited to attend, be sure to let guests know this. Use playful verbiage such as "Yes, you will need a sitter," or "This party is child-free." If the invitation indicates no children, arrange for a babysitter for your kids out of your home.

**Directions**—Type directions to your house and send them with the invitations so you won't need to write them out or say them repeatedly over the phone.

**No Surprises**—Respect people's wishes. Don't plan a surprise party for a person who has specifically stated that s/he does not want one. Not everyone is comfortable in the spotlight.

**Supplies**—If you host parties frequently, invest in folding chairs and tables. Check wholesale clubs for better prices. You might also consider purchasing a metal clothes rack for guests' coats. These can be found sometimes on sale at stores that are going out of business.

**Where's My Coat?**—Place guests' coats where they are accessible. Someone may need to retrieve a cell phone, a pack of cigarettes, or a stick of gum from a coat pocket. Also, this saves you from having to store and retrieve coats during the party.

**Renting Place Settings**— If you don't want to use paper plates and plastic utensils, and do not have enough plates and silverware of your own, check into renting them from a local rental company. You will be surprised at the low cost per place setting and you don't have to wash them!

**Amusement**—To add a little spice to the party, rent an activity from a local amusement company like a moonbounce or a Velcro wall—yes for adults! More costly, but fun and impressive, is renting a hot air balloon for tethered rides.

**Name Tags**—Use name tags when the party includes several groups of friends who do not know each other. You may want to include a little tidbit about the guest on the name tag to get conversation started between strangers.

**Decorate With Photos**—Poster-size photos are inexpensive to produce and make a great decoration for a retirement, birthday, or anniversary party. These are generally available through mail order photo services and photo processing centers.

**Decorate With Chalk**—Use colored chalk on your driveway or sidewalk to write messages for the guest of honor. Draw theme-related illustrations.

**Tablecloth**—Buy a piece of fabric to match the theme. Use pinking shears or fabric glue/tape for no-sew edges.

**Giant Greeting Card**—Make a giant hand-made greeting card out of poster board with a congratulatory message for the guest of honor. Hang it near the entrance and have everyone sign it as they arrive.

**Names on Cups**—Provide markers for people to write their names on paper cups. This helps in two ways, 1) people know where their drinks are, and 2) less waste of cups.

**Low-Fat Food**—For guests who may be watching their weight, offer a few snacks and dishes which are low in calories and made with no-fat ingredients.

**Identify Food**—Small hand-written tent cards can easily identify each dish on your buffet. People appreciate knowing what they are eating. You might also want to list the ingredients in case someone is allergic to a certain one.

**What? No cake?**—Instead of a birthday cake, serve a giant cookie. These can be purchased in bakeries or you can make one yourself. There is plenty of room on it to write and decorate with icing.

**TV Off**—The television should be turned off during a party, unless of course, you are gathering to watch a sporting event or television special.

**No Pets Allowed**—Place pets in a room separate from the party area. Some guests may be allergic, some may be afraid of pets, and some may not like pets underfoot.

**Party in the Basement**—You don't necessarily have to set up a party inside of your house. Use the garage or unfinished basement—very conducive for a rained-out cookout. First, unclutter and clean the area. The concrete floor is a great place to begin decorating; draw pictures according to your theme using colored chalk (mops up easily).

**Unique Thank You Notes**—Duplicate your party pictures and send them as thank you notes for gifts. Use them like postcards.

## *If you are the guest . . .*

**Respond!**—When you are invited to a party, consider it an honor to be included on the guest list. When an invitation indicates 'RSVP,' it is for a reason. Be considerate enough to respond—on time!

**Show Up!**—If your RSVP was affirmative, make sure you show up at the party. If you can't make it at the last minute, call the hostess and tell the truth about why you can't be there.

**Offer to Bring Something**—When responding to an invitation, ask if you can bring food or drinks. However, ask well before the party when the hostess is still planning. If you bring food, let the hostess know what dish is coming.

**Licorice Tray**—A unique treat to bring to a party is a licorice tray. Arrange all types of licorice which you can purchase in varieties of shapes and flavors: pipes, shoestring, pull-apart, sticks, bites, swirls, and squares.

**Pretzel Station**—Another yummy party treat to bring is a pretzel station. Include pretzels of many variations: sticks, wheels, thins, rods, nuggets, hard, and soft. Provide a medley of dipping delights: honey mustard, mustard, hummus, ranch dip, melted chocolate, melted cheese, and glaze.

**Chocolate Dipping**—This treat is fun and delicious! Provide a tray of items to dip into melted chocolate like pretzels, graham crackers, pineapple chunks, and strawberries. Bring along a fondue dish to keep the chocolate warm.

**Thank The Hostess**—After attending a party, send a note to the hostess indicating that you appreciated the invitation, the fun and her efforts.

**Please come to a**

**FLOWER POWER**

**PARTY**

**Corresponds with theme on page 4**. To create the flower, copy at 100% on bright colored medium/heavyweight paper. Cut out along outside lines. Fold along dotted line with printed side facing the front. Lightly mark with a pencil where the petals stop to give yourself a guideline of where to write the party details (they shouldn't show when the card is folded). Write the party details on the inside, then erase the pencil marks. Affix bee sticker (see page 4).

To make the stem, copy at 100% on green medium/heavy weight paper. Cut along outside lines. Glue area above dotted line and paste bottom of folded flower so that the dotted line is not visible. Mail in a 3-5/8 x 6-1/2" standard business envelope.

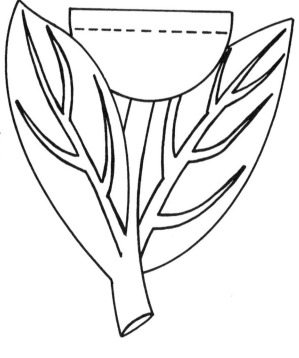

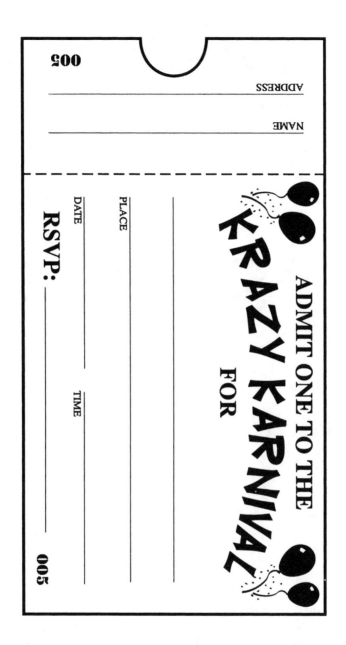

**Corresponds with theme on page 10.** Reproduce at 100% on a copy machine using white paper. Write the party information in the appropriate spaces. This will be the master copy. Reproduce the desired number of invitations on bright colored paper. A heavier weight stock like index paper works best (ask what is available at your local copy center). Cut out. Print the guest's name on the stub portion of the ticket. Add confetti or a deflated balloon in the envelope. Mail in a standard 3-5/8 x 6-1/2" business envelope.

**Corresponds with theme on page 25.** To make the fish, reproduce this design on a copy machine at 100% on medium/heavyweight colored paper. Cut out along outside lines. Cut small triangles or tear small pieces of various colored tissue paper. Starting near the tail, glue rows of "scales" to the fish body. Refer to the illustration on page 25. Tie a 5" piece of fishing line to a small silver paper clip and insert the paper clip into the fish's mouth. To make bubbles, reproduce the circles at 100% on a sheet of white paper. Fill in the appropriate party details; this will be the master copy. Copy at 100% on light blue medium/heavy weight paper. Cut out the individual bubbles and enclose along with the fish in a 5-1/2 x 4-3/8" invitation envelope. Or, arrange the circles as shown on page 25 and glue bubbles to each other to appear as though they are coming out of the fish's mouth (make sure that the finished product will fit in the envelope).

cut out this black circle and discard

You're **BUGGIN' ME!** PARTY

pattern for Mylar piece

**Corresponds with theme on page 29.** On a copy machine, reproduce this design at 130% on white paper. Rubber cement the entire piece of white paper onto a piece of gray construction paper. (This enables the outside of the magnifying glass to be gray while the inside remains white.) Cut out magnifying glass along outside lines. Cut out black circle and discard. Using the Mylar pattern, cut pieces of Mylar or other clear plastic and place along dotted circle of the magnifying glass. Tape in place. Fold at dotted line with the words on the inside. Glue the halves of the magnifying glass together around the perimeter only. Add party details on the front handle with a fine tip marker. Place bug stickers where desired. Mail in 5-1/2 x 4-3/8" invitation envelopes.

PLACE:

RSVP:

TIME:

DATE:

Come CELEBRATE!

It's

BIRTHDAY!

Join the safari,
Blend in well,
Khaki and animal prints
Sure would be swell!

**Corresponds with theme on page 39.** On a copy machine, reproduce this design at 135% on white paper. This will be the master copy. Using a black fine tip marker, print the party details in the appropriate spaces. Reproduce from the master copy as many copies as desired at 100% on a different colored medium weight paper for each animal. Or, select beige paper to resemble real animal crackers. Cut out each animal shape. Purchase animal cracker boxes and empty the cookies. (Maybe you can use them at the party.) Include a set of party animals in each box. Place a label on the outside of the box with the guest's name and address; then mail or hand deliver. If mailing, add a spot of hot glue on the lid so it doesn't open in transit.

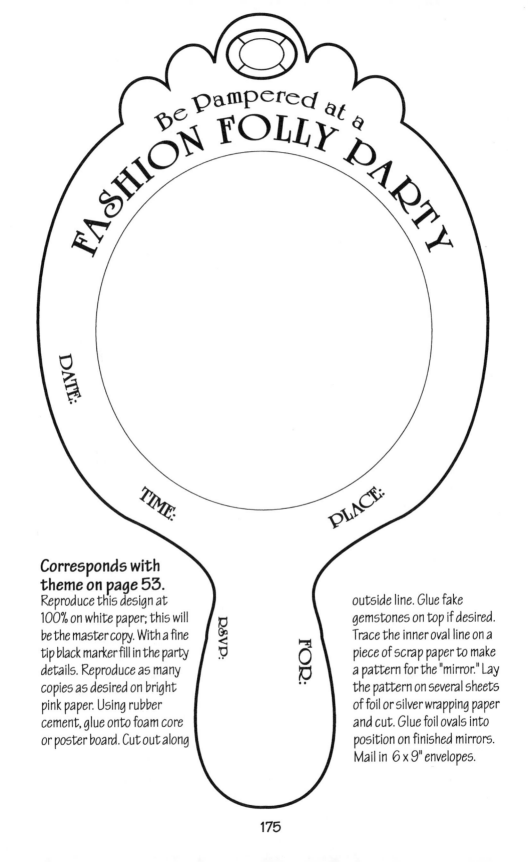

Be Pampered at a

FASHION FOLLY PARTY

DATE:

TIME:

PLACE:

R&VP:

FOR:

**Corresponds with theme on page 53.**
Reproduce this design at 100% on white paper; this will be the master copy. With a fine tip black marker fill in the party details. Reproduce as many copies as desired on bright pink paper. Using rubber cement, glue onto foam core or poster board. Cut out along outside line. Glue fake gemstones on top if desired. Trace the inner oval line on a piece of scrap paper to make a pattern for the "mirror." Lay the pattern on several sheets of foil or silver wrapping paper and cut. Glue foil ovals into position on finished mirrors. Mail in 6 x 9" envelopes.

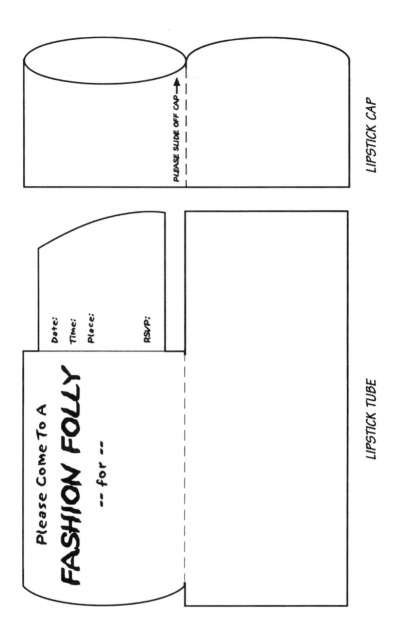

**LIPSTICK CAP**

PLEASE SLIDE OFF CAP →

Date:
Time:
Place:

RSVP:

Please Come To A
FASHION FOLLY
-- for --

**LIPSTICK TUBE**

**Corresponds with theme on page 53.** On a copy machine, reproduce this design at 100% on white paper; this will be the master copy. With a fine tip black marker fill in the party details. Reproduce at 200% from the master copy as many copies as desired on bright pink, red or purple paper. (The cap and the lipstick will have to be reproduced separately since when enlarged they will not fit on one 8-1/2 x 11" sheet of paper.) For the lipstick tube, fold along dotted line with the words on the outside. Glue the halves together and cut along bold lines. For the lipstick cap, fold along dotted line and cut along bold lines. Place a fine line of glue along top and left side, but do not glue along straight edge (needs to be open to place over lipstick tube). Mail assembled invitation in a standard 4-1/8 x 9-1/2" standard business envelope. Have the birthday girl put on lipstick and kiss the sealed envelope!

176

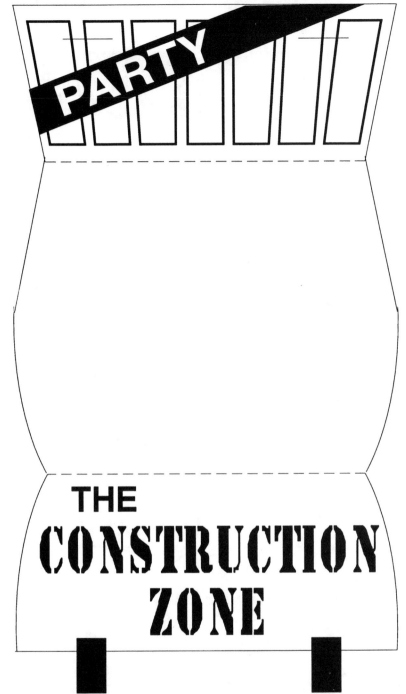

**Corresponds with theme on page 57.** On a copy machine, reproduce as many copies as desired of this design at 120% on yellow medium/heavyweight paper. Cut around outside solid lines. With an exacto knife, slice the two short horizontal lines on either side of the word "party." (This will allow the tabs to be inserted to keep the top panel of the finished lunch box closed.) Fold at the dotted lines so that the words are on the outside of the lunch box. Run a thin line of glue along the two side edges of the "party" flap and seal (this creates a pocket on the inside of the lunch box). Refer to the illustrations on page 57.

YIELD TO THE FUN ZONE!

Print your last name here

_____ CREW:
PLEASE REPORT TO THE
FUN ZONE AT_____ SHARP
WEARING A WHITE T-SHIRT
AND JEANS.
QUITTING TIME IS_____

Print beginning and ending times here

DATE

RSVP

COME CELEBRATE! ITS

_____

_____

BIRTHDAY!

**Corresponds with theme on page 57.** On a copy machine, reproduce this design at 100% on white paper. This will be the master copy. Using a black fine tip marker, print the party details in the appropriate spaces. Reproduce from the master copy as many sets as desired at 100% on colored medium weight paper (red for the apple, tan for the sandwich, blue for the thermos). Cut out along outside lines. Insert a set in the pocket of each lunch box. Enlarge the "FUN ZONE" banner 120% on white paper. Cut and paste the banner on the top panel of the inside of the lunch box. Refer to illustrations on page 57. Mail assembled lunch box in a 5-1/2 x 4-3/8" invitation envelope.

# HELLO
# HAPPY CAMPER!

## YOU'RE INVITED TO PITCH A TENT AT

## CAMP

**Date:** _____    **Place:** _____

**Time:** _____    _____

RSVP TO CAMP COUNSELOR _____ @ _____

**Corresponds with theme on page 62.** To create an 8-1/2 x 11" flyer, make a 165% enlargement of this design on a copy machine. Print your personal information in the appropriate spaces. Blank space is provided to add other details like directions, specific items to bring, etc. Follow delivery suggestions on page 62, or fold and mail in standard 4-1/8 x 9-1/2" business envelopes.

Uncle Sam wants **YOU**
to join the fun at
# BOOT CAMP

Please report to duty on:

Official time:

RSVP:

You will be stationed at:

**Corresponds with theme on page 72.** To create the boot, copy at 100% on light brown or army green medium/heavy weight paper. Copy two for every invitation needed. Cut out along outside lines. Place a thin line of glue along outside edges except for the top (this is where the Uncle Sam card will be inserted). Hole punch the shoe string holes; lace with real shoe strings, ribbon or string, and tie in a bow. To make the card, fill in the party details, and write your child's name in front of BOOT CAMP. Copy at 100% on white index paper. Trim along outside lines and insert in boot.
Mail in a 5-1/2 x 4-3/8" invitation envelope.

**Corresponds with theme on page 76.** On a copy machine, reproduce this design at 100% on white paper. With a black fine tip marker, fill in the appropriate party details (leave room for stickers as shown on page 76) and write your child's name on the tea bag tag. This will be the master copy. Reproduce as many copies as desired on pastel paper. Cut out the same number of plain tea cup shapes, also on pastel paper, to use for the backs. On the printed version, cut a slot slightly larger than the width of a real tea bag so a tea bag can be inserted into the slot. Glue the printed design of the cup on top of a blank tea cup shape, along the outside edges only. Affix teddy bear and/or flower stickers to the tea cup. Staple the personalized tea bag tag onto the string of the tea bag and insert the tea bag into the slot in the cup. Additional party details may be printed on the back of the tag or cup. Mail in 5-1/2" x 4-3/8" invitation envelopes.

**Corresponds with theme on page 80.** To create an 8-1/2 x 11" flyer, make a 165% enlargement of this design on a copy machine. Print the party details in the appropriate spaces. Blank space is provided to add further details, like directions, specific items to bring, etc. Reproduce the desired amount of copies and roll up as directed on page 80, or fold and mail in standard 4-1/8 x 9-1/2" business envelopes.

**Corresponds with theme on page 85.** On a copy machine, reproduce this design at 100% on white paper. This will be the master copy. Using a black fine tip marker, print the appropriate party details as shown on the illustration on page 85. Reproduce as many copies as desired at 100% on colored medium/heavyweight paper. If desired, attach a real toothbrush with hot glue or tacky glue as shown on page 85. Mail in a 6 x 9" envelope.

**Corresponds with theme on page 89.** To make apron & hat, reproduce this design on a copy machine at 100% on white paper. You will need one hat and one apron for each invitation. Cut out individually. To make gingerbread men, cut out design to use as a pattern. Cut a 17-1/2 x 5" rectangle from a large brown paper grocery bag. Fold accordion style making four panels, each measuring 4-3/8" wide x 5" high. Position pattern on top panel and trace with a pencil. With panels folded, cut gingerbread man along tracing, making certain that you do not cut where the arms and legs touch the sides (to keep the four connected when panels are opened). Open the strand of gingerbread men and decorate the far left one with fine tip colored markers. Cut two 6" pieces of 1/8" wide satin ribbon. Using tacky glue, adhere one end of each piece of ribbon to the waist on the front cookie. Then glue the apron on top of the ribbon; likewise glue the hat on the head. Open the gingerbread men with the front one facing up and print the party details on the middle two panels. Fold up and tie the ribbons in a bow at the back panel. See page 89. Mail in a 5-1/2 x 4-3/8" invitation envelope.

184

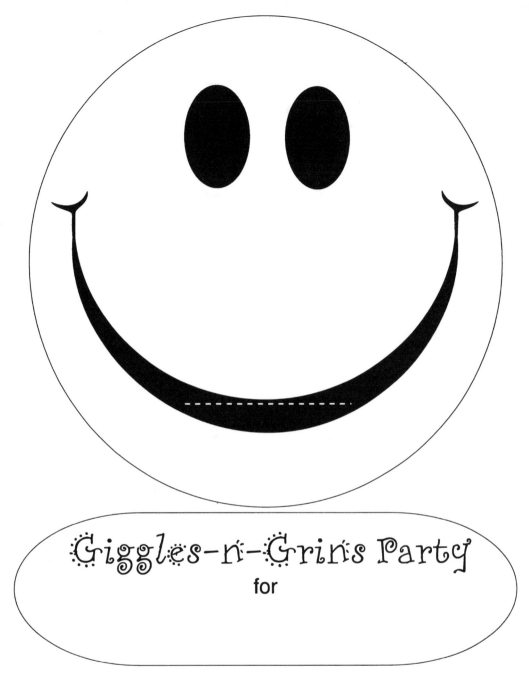

**Giggles-n-Grins Party**

for

**Corresponds with theme on page 94.** To make the smiley face, reproduce at 100% on a copier using bright yellow paper. Cut along outside circle. Also cut the same number of plain yellow circles for the backs. Using an exacto knife, cut along the white dotted line in the smile for the tongue to be inserted. Place a smiley face on top of a plain circle and glue around entire circumference (not in the middle area; make sure the dotted line has been cut before gluing). To make the tongue, write the name of the birthday child on it and reproduce at 100% using bright pink paper. Cut out. Print party specifics either on back of the tongues or on the backs of faces. Insert a tongue in each smiley face, letting it stick out partially. Mail in 6 x 9" envelopes.

**Corresponds with theme on page 94.** Reproduce at
130% on a copier using white paper. Write the party information following
the contours of the design as shown on page 94. This will be the master
copy. Reproduce the desired number of invitations on bright paper. A
heavier weight stock like index paper works best (ask what is available
at your local copy center). Cut out around the outside lines. Mail in a
standard 4-1/8 x 9-1/2" business envelope.

# Index

# Meet the Party Girl . . .

Photo by Hal Hagy

Suzanne Molino Singleton established Twenty-Nine Angels Publishing, LLC in 1997 to produce her first book, **Clever Gift Giving.**

**Clever Party Planning** is her second spin as an author. Suzanne plans to continue writing a series of "clever" books, with the next one already written, **Clever Costume Creating**. Although her publishing company is young, Suzanne has plans for its growth, including the publishing of a novel and two children's books, also already written. Several other books by Suzanne await their turn at being published as Twenty-Nine Angels Publishing unfolds.

Suzanne's party enthusiasm is based on ideas she learned as a special event planner and public relations specialist in the corporate world, a Girl Scout leader for seven years, a mother of two young children for seven years, and a daughter of a quite creative mom for 39 years!

She creates from an office in her home in Maryland while raising her two kiddies and two twenty-something stepsons. She is married to Ken Singleton, a baseball announcer for the New York Yankees and a retired Baltimore Oriole.

Suzanne's life is greatly assisted by angels which is why she believes in them, collects them, talks to them, and includes them everywhere.

She thanks you wholeheartedly for buying this book!

# Notes

# Notes

# Notes

# Notes

# Notes

# Notes

# Notes

## *other books by*
# Suzanne Singleton

Photo by Publisher's Photographic Services

### *Clever Gift Giving* . . . . . . . **$9.95**
Shipping (each book) . . . . . . . . . . . . 2.50
ISBN # 0-9661253-0-4, softcover,
80 pages

Give a unique gift that can be the hit of the party! Over 300 fresh and clever ideas are yours for housewarming, theme gifts, wedding shower, showing thanks, giving to your teens and tots, and more! Clever Gift Giving is packed with inventive gift ideas, party tips, wrapping hints and inspirational quotes. This whimsical handbook is guaranteed to jump start your creativing in gift giving!

## Coming Spring 2000 . . .
### Clever Costume Creating
This A to Z guide provides over 150 ideas for no-sew adult Halloween costumes. You'll find a clever costume to create for your group or yourself to celebrate that wacky Halloween season!
ISBN #0-9661253-3-9

# To Order . . .

By credit card . . . call Twenty-Nine Angels Publishing LLC @ 410-771-4821 or out of state @ 1-800-736-7729 during regular business hours (EST). Major credit cards accepted.

By mail . . . send a check or money order payable to Twenty-Nine Angels Publishing to P.O. Box 907, Sparks, Maryland, 21152-9300. Current shipping and handling charges will apply. Maryland residents please add 5% sales tax.